THE KETO DIET COOKBOOK FOR BEGINNERS

Easy & Delicious Low Carb Recipes for Busy People on Keto Diet

(Keto Diet for Beginners)

Francis Michael

COPYRIGHT © 2020 by Francis Michael

ISBN: 978-1-952504-13-6

All rights reserved. This book is copyright protected and it's for personal use only. Without the prior written permission of the publisher, no part of this publication should be reproduced, distributed, or transmitted in any form or by any means, including photocopying, recording, or other electronic or mechanical methods. This publication is sold with the idea that the publisher is not required to render accounting, officially permitted, or otherwise, qualified services. Seek for the services of a legal or professional, a practiced individual in the profession if advice is needed.

DISCLAIMER

The information contained in this book is geared for educational and entertainment purposes only. Strenuous efforts have been made towards providing accurate, up to date and reliable complete information. The information in this book is true and complete to the best of our knowledge. Neither the publisher nor the author takes any responsibility for any possible consequences of reading or enjoying the recipes in this book. The author and publisher disclaim any liability in connection with the use of information contained in this book. Under no circumstance will any legal responsibility or blame be apportioned against the author or publisher for any reparation, damages, or monetary loss due to the information herein, either directly or indirectly.

Table of Contents

INTRODUCTION 9

What Is Keto Diet 9

How Does the Keto Diet Work 10

Benefits of Keto Diet 11

How to Kick-Start Ketosis 12

What are Carbs 13

Foods That Are High In Carbs 14

Foods to Eat On Keto Diet 16

Foods to Avoid On Keto Diet 17

Tips for Achieving Success on Keto Diet 18

Tips for Eating Out On Keto Diet 19

KETO DIET SMOOTHIES & BREAKFAST RECIPES 20

    Peppermint Smoothie 20

    Homemade Sage Sausage Patties 21

    Strawberry Smoothie 22

    Strawberry Avocado Smoothie 23

    Brunch-Style Portobello Mushrooms 24

    Egg-tastic Smoothie 25

    Raspberry Cheesecake Smoothie 26

    Savory Apple-Chicken Sausage 27

    Cool Hazelnut Smoothie 28

    Salt and Caramel Smoothie 29

    Spiced Chai Latte 30

    Strawberry and Rhubarb Pie Smoothie 31

    Mini Spinach Frittatas 32

Strawberry Coco Smoothie ... 33

Rosemary Keto Bagels ... 34

Strawberry and Black Currant Smoothie ... 35

Coconut Macadamia Bars ... 36

Blueberry Smoothie ... 37

Buttery Coconut Flour Waffles ... 38

Avocado Raspberry Chocolate Smoothie ... 39

Orange Peel and Ginger Lassi ... 40

Rooibos Tea Latte ... 41

KETO DIET BRUNCH & DINNER RECIPES ... 42

Simple Shrimp Ceviche ... 42

Baked Pork Chops ... 43

Garlic Parmesan Zucchini Pasta ... 45

Garlic and Herb Pork Loin Roast ... 46

Chicken and Veggie Shish Kabob ... 47

Chicken Salad with Peach Balsamic Dressing ... 48

Midday Boost Latte ... 50

BBQ Ranch Burgers ... 51

Crack Slaw ... 52

Shrimp Stir Fry with Baked Cauliflower Rice ... 53

Mushroom Bacon Skillet ... 54

Curry Chicken Lettuce Wraps ... 55

Roasted Chicken Stacks ... 56

Keto Chili ... 57

Lemon Herb Meatloaf ... 58

White Turkey Chili ... 59

 Loaded Cauliflower Bake 60

KETO DIET POULTRY RECIPES 61

 Grilled Chicken Caesar Salad 61

 Caprese Chicken Mozzarella 63

 BBQ Chicken Crust Pizza 64

 Chicken Schnitzel a La Holstein 65

 Buffalo Chicken Dip... 66

 Homemade Sloppy Joes 67

 Mexican Chicken Casserole 68

 Chicken Enchilada Dip 70

 Chicken Pizza Crust 71

 Spinach Strawberry Pecan Salad 72

 Smoked Chicken Leg Quarters 74

 Tangy Ranch Chicken Wings.. 75

 Chicken Cordon Bleu Casserole... 76

 Chicken Tenders 77

 Chicken Alfredo Casserole with Broccoli 78

 Chicken Tikka Masala 80

 Chicken Bacon Ranch Casserole 82

 Caprese Hassel-back Chicken 83

KETO DIET SOUP, STEW & SALAD RECIPES 84

 Keto Chicken and Cabbage Stew 84

 Southern Potlikker Soup 85

 Thai Tom Sap Pork Ribs Soup 86

 Egg Drop Soup 87

 One-Pot Beef Stew.. 88

- Asian Chicken Meatball Soup 89
- Chicken Cobb Salad with Cobb Salad Dressing 91
- Spinach Strawberry Pecan Salad 92
- Greek Salad 94
- Sweet Bell Pepper Salad 96
- Cucumber Salad 97
- Tzatziki Sauce 98
- Homemade Ranch Seasoning 99
- Spinach Salad with Warm Bacon Dressing 100
- Honey Mustard Dressing and Dipping Sauce 102
- Cauliflower Tabbouleh 103
- Grilled Chicken Caesar Salad 104

KETO DIET BEEF & PORK RECIPES 105

- Lebanese Hashweh Ground Beef and Rice 105
- Beef Kheema Meatloaf 107
- Beef Shawarma 108
- Spicy Ground Pork Stir Fry 109
- Mexican Zucchini and Beef 111
- Korean Ground Beef 112
- Cheeseburger and Cauliflower 113
- Ground Beef Casserole 114
- Salad Healthy Taco with Ground Beef 116

KETO DIET FISH & SEAFOOD RECIPES 117

- Mini Fish Cakes 117
- Chinese Petrale Sole with Ginger and Garlic 118
- Easy Sardines Salad 119

Sardines and Onions 120

Italian Tuna Salad 121

Coconut Tuna Fish Cakes 122

Curried Tuna Salad 123

Tomato Tuna Bruschetta 124

Pink Peppercorn Smoked Salmon Salad 125

Baked Rosemary Salmon 126

Creamy Salmon Pasta 127

Bacon-Wrapped Salmon 128

Salmon Curry 129

Garlic Shrimp Caesar Salad 130

Shrimp Cocktail 132

KETO DIET VEGETARIAN & VEGAN RECIPES 133

Cauliflower Toast 133

Baked Egg Avocado Boats 134

Creamy Avocado Dip 135

Jalapeño Popper Bread 136

Triple Berry Smoothie 137

Almond Flour Waffles 138

Chocolate Protein Shake 139

Fat Bombs 140

Easy Cereal 141

Cheesy Cauliflower Breadsticks 143

Bell Pepper Nachos 144

Avocado Pesto and Spaghetti Squash 146

Cumin Cilantro Cauliflower Rice 147

- Easy Roasted Broccoli 148
- Cheesy Garlic Roasted Asparagus 149

KETO DIET APPETIZER RECIPES 150

- Crunchy Rosemary Crackers 150
- Macadamia Nut Hummus 151
- Cauliflower Mac and Cheese 152
- Cheesy Buffalo Chicken Dip 153
- Chipotle Red Pepper Cheese Dip 154
- Epic Charcuterie Board 155
- General Tso's Meatballs 157
- Pepperoni Pizza Stuffed Mushrooms 159
- Cheese Tray-Cheddar, Monterey Jack, and Cream Cheese Platter 160
- Eggplant Tomato Mini Pizza 162
- Creamy Herb and Cucumber Dressing 163

INTRODUCTION

What Is Keto Diet

When talking about Keto Diet, it's simply a short form for Ketogenic Diet. The diet has to do much with a low-carb (carbohydrate) meal. This means the process of lowering intake of carbohydrates and increasing the intake of fat. This leads to fat being turn into ketones. The Ketones in turn supplies the human brain with energy. It also involves much intake of fats, veggies and proteins etc. Keto Diet however helps to burn fats instead of burning carbohydrates. Carbohydrates are converted into glucose which in turn helps to energies the human brain. If small amount of carbohydrates are contain in a particular diet, the liver converts fat into fatty acids and ketone bodies.

How Does the Keto Diet Work

In reality, Keto Diet places it emphases on fat which make up to about 95%nof daily calories. The human body in the other hand makes use of different types of fuel for its healthy living. The keto Diet is capable of providing the human body diverse kinds of fuel. This fuel is known as Ketone. The Liver uses stored fat to manufacture this Ketone. The Keto Diet works perfectly well if one follows it instructions properly. The Keto Diet in the other hand needs you to deny yourself intake of carbohydrates. Reaching A state called Ketosis may take some few days but this can be interfered when you consume too much protein.

Benefits of Keto Diet

Keto Diet can be beneficial in the following ways:

1. **It Controls your cravings:**

This can be possible when you control your general blood sugar levels helps you control your cravings. Several studies have revealed this to be truth.

2. **Keto Diet sharpens your brain:**

Keto Diet helps to sharpen the human brain and fuel it when glucose is absence. The brain also gets energies through the Keto diet.

3. **It helps to fall the Inflammation markers:**

Studies reveal that cases of inflammation come as a result of diverse health issues like diabetes, heart disease, and arthritis etc. The nutritional values of Ketosis have the capability to reduce inflammation.

4. **You are safe from type 2 diabetes:**

A study reveals that Keto Diet can improve blood sugar control for people living with type 2 diabetes. Being on Ketosis can drastically reduce your daily carbohydrates to less than 20g. This helps to manage or control the condition of the type 2 diabetes.

5. **It gives the human body more energy:**

Keto Diet is equipped with the ability of proving energy to the body. For those who are new to Keto Diet may experience Keto flu during the first few days of being on Keto Diet. Some may have fatigue, headaches, and nausea. When this happens, it simply connotes that your body is setting up itself from the usual burning of glucose to burning of fat for energy. Your body will gain more energy when it is fully switched.

How to Kick-Start Ketosis

The Keto Diet is all about setting up your body to start burning fat instead of glucose when energy is needed by the body.

The keto Diet comprises of low carb (carbohydrate), and high fat diets. The Keto Diet has become popular in most parts of the globe because people have now come to like it due to its numerous health benefits. Starting the Keto diet is very simple but some people do have some doubt in them asking themselves if the keto Diet can work in them as it works for others. Starting The Keto Diet also requires that you know what Keto Diet is so that kick start with ease. Kick starting Ketosis could include: cutting down carbohydrates intake, eating high-quality fats, doing much exercise, maintaining your protein level.

What are Carbs

One of the ways in which the body obtains calories is through carbohydrates being are macronutrients. Carbs is a short form of saying carbohydrate while calories also mean energy. Carbohydrates according to several studies show that carbohydrate is the main source of energy. Carbohydrate is a combination of carbon, hydrogen and oxygen. That is why they are called carbohydrate. Normally, the daily consumption of 1g of carbohydrate is equivalent to 4 calories. This means a diet of 1,800 calories per day will give about 202g and 292g for both low and high end.

Foods That Are High In Carbs

1. **Black Beans:**

Beans are known to contain protein and fiber but they however contain traces of carbohydrates.

2. **Whole Wheat Pasta:**

Whole wheat pasta contains a whole lot of carbs necessary for your body to get into Ketosis.

3. **Yogurt:**

It may interest you to know that yogurt is high in carbohydrate. Yes sure, it is.

4. **Maple Syrup:**

This is also a good source of carbohydrates despite the fact that they are sweetener, they also contains carbohydrates.

5. **Dates:**

Their sizes are not necessary but they are a good source of carbohydrates.

6. **Corn:**

Corn is stock with lots of carbohydrates which give more energy to the body for a healthy living.

7. **Quinoa:**

They have traces of carbohydrates in their nutritional content. It's a good source of carbohydrate.

8. **Adzuki Beans:**

These Asian beans. It origin come from China according to research. It is also a good source of carbohydrates.

9. **Chickpeas:**

Chickpeas are high in carbohydrates. They are the main ingredient in hummus. They contain high level of carbohydrates.

10. **Grapefruit:**

This citrus contains a good amount of carbohydrates.

11. **Oats:**

Oats are good example of food that is high in carbohydrates. Many people begin their morning with oats.

12. **Sweet Potatoes:**

Sweet potatoes are another source of carbohydrate. Although sweet potatoes contains lower carbs compared to the white potatoes.

Foods to Eat On Keto Diet

1. **Beef:**

Roast, Steak, veal, ground beef and stews

2. **Poultry:**

Quail, duck, Chicken breasts, turkey and wild game

3. **Pork:**

Tenderloin, Pork loin, chops, ham, and sugar-free bacon

4. **Fish:**

Tuna, salmon, Mackerel trout, halibut, cod, catfish, and mahi-mahi

5. **Shellfish:**

Clams, crab, Oysters, mussels, and lobster

6. **Organ meats:**

Liver, tongue, Heart, kidney, and offal

7. **Eggs:**

Fried, deviled, scrambled and boiled

8. **Leafy greens:**

Spinach, Kale, Swiss chard and arugula

9. **Cruciferous vegetables:**

Cauliflower, Cabbage, and zucchini

10. **Lettuces:**

Romaine, Iceberg, and butter-head

11. **Oil:**

Coconut butter, Coconut oil, Flaxseed oil, Olive oil, Sesame seed oil, MCT oil, Walnut oil, avocado oil, Heavy cream and heavy whipping cream

Foods to Avoid On Keto Diet

1. **Grains:**

These are good sources of carbohydrates. When you are on Keto Diet, the best thing to do is to avoid foods that are grains. These include wheat; pasta, whole grains, rice, quinoa, oats, barley, rye, and corn.

2. **Sugar:**

Avoid eating sugary things like artificial smoothies, sweeteners, soda, and fruit juice, ketchup and BBQ. They are all sauces of sugar, so avoid them.

3. **Alcohol:**

The major content of alcohol is ethanol. This can stop your body from producing ketones. So avoid intake of alcohol. Some beverages contain alcohol.

4. **Starchy Veggies:**

When you are on Keto Diet, try to avoid starchy vegetables for examples sweet potatoes, some squash, potatoes, parsnips, and carrots. Instead you may choose to like taking fruits as they are more beneficial in Keto Diets.

5. **Seed Oils:**

When you heat seed oils in a skillet, they can become oxidized. You need to completely do away with canola oil, corn oil, and peanut oil. They are good source of omega 6 fatty acids. The acid could be inflammatory when they are in large amounts.

6. **Beans and Legumes:**

Beans and legumes are very high in carbohydrate. You need to avoid consuming food like chickpeas, black beans, lentils and kidney beans.

Tips for Achieving Success on Keto Diet

1. **Make Use of Exogenous Ketones:**

This also helps to stick to Keto Diet because it is equivalent to MCT oil. Taking exogenous ketones is just a short way to get into ketosis.

2. **Count Your Carbohydrates:**

It is pertinent to adapt to a system of counting or measuring your daily intake of carbohydrate. You have to be very mindful because there are some hidden carbohydrates in some foods which may look Keto friendly but absolutely contain sugar. Such foods include the following: Milk, Chicken wings loaded with barbecue, blueberries, yogurt, breaded meats etc.

3. **Improve your Gut Micro-biome:**

Every human system is linked to gut health. Human gut micro-biome affects everything ranging from the mental health to the digestive system and many other systems found in the human body. When your gut flora is healthy, the metabolic flexibility, hormones, and insulin sensitivity in the body become more efficient and effective. When the body need to utilized energy, the above process can have an effect in your ability to change from carbohydrates to fats for energy. This help to achieve success on Keto Diet.

4. **Clear Out Your Kitchen:**

It is very important to make sure your kitchen is properly clean after every meal you prepare. This will make you convenient and prepare healthy meal. When your kitchen is clean, you will be highly compelled to stick to the Keto Diet. Replacing all of your carbs, except for non-starchy vegetables, with keto-friendly foods will help you stick to Keto Diet.

5. **Always Have Convenient Snacks On Hand:**

Concentrating on the Keto Diet needs time. Some people gets discouraged because of the lots of foods you need to prepare. In the absence of enough time, the alternative is to make lots of keto-friendly or carb heavy snacks when you have limited time. Such snacks include: Hard boiled eggs, Beef jerky, premade guacamole.

Tips for Eating Out On Keto Diet

New people on Keto Diet may find it difficult to identify foods that are Keto friendly and foods that are not Keto friendly. It is important to identify and know those Keto friendly foods while you are eating out. You do not need to eat anything you see out there. Most of the restaurants you will visit have a whole lot of Keto friendly foods which will prompt you to make your choice. Below are guidelines on how to stick to Keto Diet when you eat outside in the restaurant:

1. **Breakfast:**

If you are eating your breakfast in a restaurant, choose eggs and bacon and green salad on the sides regularly. This can substitute pancakes or toast.

2. **Lunch:**

Lunch is always alternatives to salad in some big restaurants. You can always replace the sugar filled dressings with vinegar or olive oil.

3. **Dinner:**

Almost all the restaurant will have meat-filled food. If you are eating your dinner in a restaurant, try to demand for their fattiest cut of steak like rib eye. You can as well replace the potatoes with vegetables. These tips help you stick to Keto Diet.

KETO DIET SMOOTHIES & BREAKFAST RECIPES

Peppermint Smoothie

Preparation Time: 5 minutes

Total Time: 5 minutes

Serves: 2

Ingredients:

- A handful of spinach
- A handful of ice
- 1 Cup of unsweetened coconut milk
- 1 Cup of unsweetened cashew milk
- ¼ Tsp. mint extract

Cooking Instructions:

1. In a food blender, combine all the ingredients and give it a perfect blend.
2. Pour the blended mixture into a glass and top with mint leaves.
3. Serve and enjoy!!!

Homemade Sage Sausage Patties

Preparation time: 10 minutes

Cook time: 15 minutes

Total time:

Ingredients:

- 1 lb. of ground pork
- ¾ cup of shredded cheddar cheese
- ¼ cup of buttermilk
- 1 tbsp. of finely chopped onion
- 2 tsp. of rubbed sage
- ¾ tsp. of salt
- ¾ tsp. of pepper
- 1/8 tsp. of garlic powder
- 1/8 tsp. of dried oregano

Cooking Instructions:

1. In a medium bowl, combine together the ingredients and give everything a good mix. Shape the mixture into eight 1/2-in.-thick patties.
2. Refrigerate for at least 1 hour. In a skillet, cook the patties over medium heat until a thermometer reads 160° for about 6-8 minutes on each side.
3. Serve and enjoy!

Strawberry Smoothie

Preparation Time: 7 minutes

Total Time: 7 minutes

Serves: 1

Ingredients:

- 2 Tbsp. heavy cream
- 1 Fresh sage leaf
- 1 Cup of unsweetened coconut milk
- 1 Tbsp. vanilla extract
- 5 Frozen strawberries

Cooking Instructions:

1. Put all the ingredients into a food processor and give it a good blend to your desired consistency.
2. Pour the blended mixture into a glass and top with fresh strawberries.
3. Serve and enjoy!!!

Strawberry Avocado Smoothie

Preparation Time: 5 minutes

Total Time: 5 minutes

Serves: 2

Ingredients:

- 2/3 Cup of unsweetened strawberries
- Stevia syrup
- 1 Ripe avocado, peeled
- ½ Cup of coconut milk
- 1 Tbsp. lemon juice

Cooking Instructions:

1. In a food blender, combine all the ingredients together and blend it properly.
2. Pour into two glasses.
3. Serve and enjoy!!!

Brunch-Style Portobello Mushrooms

Prep/Total Time: 30 min.

Yield: 4

Ingredients:

- 4 large Portobello mushrooms, stems removed
- 2 packages (10 oz. each) frozen creamed spinach, thawed
- 4 large eggs
- ¼ cup of shredded Gouda cheese
- ½ cup of crumbled cooked bacon
- Salt and pepper, optional

Cooking Instructions:

1. Add the mushrooms, stem side up, in baking pan. Spoon spinach onto mushrooms and crack an egg into the middle of each mushroom.
2. Sprinkle the mushroom with cheese and bacon. Bake at 375°F for 18-20 minutes. Sprinkle with salt and pepper if desired.
3. Serve and enjoy!

Egg-tastic Smoothie

Preparation Time: 5 minutes

Total Time: 5 minutes

Serves: 1

Ingredients:

- 3 Ice cubes
- ¼ Cup of Heavy cream
- 2 Raw eggs
- 2 Tbsp. Cream cheese
- 1 Tsp. Vanilla extract

Cooking Instructions:

1. Beat the eggs into a food blender and give it a good blend.
2. Pour in all the remaining ingredients and continue blending to have a smooth mixture.
3. Pour the blended mixture into a glass and top with heavy cream.
4. Serve and enjoy!!!

Raspberry Cheesecake Smoothie

Preparation Time: 5 minutes

Total Time: 5 minutes

Serves: 1

Ingredients:

- 1 Oz. Cream cheese
- 1 Tbsp. Vanilla extract
- ½ Cup of Raspberries
- 1 Cup of Almonds

Cooking Instructions:

1. Put all the ingredients into a food processor and give it a good blend to your desired consistency.
2. Pour the blended mixture into a glass and top with fresh raspberries.
3. Serve and enjoy!!!

Savory Apple-Chicken Sausage

Prep/Total Time: 25 minutes

Yield: 8 patties

Ingredients:

- 1 large tart apple, peeled and diced
- 2 tsp. of poultry seasoning
- 1 tsp. of salt
- ¼ tsp. of pepper
- 1 lb. of ground chicken

Cooking Instructions:

1. In a medium bowl, combine together the apple, poultry seasoning, salt and pepper. Crumble chicken over mixture and give everything a good mix.
2. Shape the mixture into eight 3-in. patties. In a greased skillet, cook patties for about 6 minutes over medium heat or until no longer pink on each side.
3. Serve and enjoy!

Cool Hazelnut Smoothie

Preparation Time: 7 minutes

Total Time: 7 minutes

Serves: 1

Ingredients:

- 1 Cup of cold coffee
- A handful of ice cubes
- 1/3 Cup of heavy cream
- 1 Tbsp. sugar-free hazelnut syrup

Cooking Instructions:

1. Put all the ingredients into a food blender and give it a good blend until it gets to your desired consistency.
2. Pour the blended mixture into a glass and top with whipped cream.
3. Serve and enjoy!!!

Salt and Caramel Smoothie

Preparation Time: 10 minutes

Total Time: 10 minutes

Serves: 1

Ingredients:

- 1 Tbsp. salted caramel syrup
- A Dash of pumpkin pie spice
- 3 Tbsp. heavy cream
- 1 Cup of unsweetened cashew milk
- 1 Handful of ice cubes

Cooking Instructions:

1. Put all the ingredients into a food blender. Start blending to your desired consistency.
2. Pour the blended mixture into a glass and top with pumpkin pie smoothie.
3. Serve and enjoy!!!

Spiced Chai Latte

Preparation Time: 5 minutes

Total Time: 5 minutes

Serves: 2

Ingredients:

- 1 Tbsp. gelatin
- 1 Tsp. cinnamon
- ½ Tsp. turmeric
- 1 Tsp. Nutmeg
- ½ Tsp. clove
- ½ Tsp. ginger
- 2 Pinches of cardamom
- Sweetener of choice to taste
- 2 Tbsp. grass-fed butter or ghee
- 1 Scoop of Vanilla Collagen Protein Powder
- 10 Oz. hot water

Cooking Instructions:

1. Put all the ingredients in a saucepan.
2. Use low heat to make the gelatin dissolved completely.
3. Empty into a blender and blend, and then pour into 2 small cups.
4. Serve and enjoy!!!

Strawberry and Rhubarb Pie Smoothie

Preparation Time: 10 minutes

Total Time: 10 minutes

Serves: 4

Ingredients:

- ½ Cup of unsweetened almond milk
- 2 Tbsp. full-fat cream
- 1 Tsp. freshly grated ginger root
- ½ Tsp. pure vanilla bean extract
- 6 Drops of stevia syrup
- 4 Medium-sized strawberries
- 2 Medium-sized rhubarb stalks
- 1 Oz. Almond
- 1 Large-sized Organic egg

Cooking Instructions:

1. Combine all the ingredients in a blender, and process.
2. Empty into a glass.
3. Serve and enjoy!!!

Mini Spinach Frittatas

Prep/Total Time: 30 minute

Yield: 2 dozen

Ingredients:

- 1 cup of whole-milk ricotta cheese
- ¾ cup of grated Parmesan cheese
- 2/3 cup of chopped fresh mushrooms
- 1 package (10 oz.) frozen chopped spinach, thawed and squeezed dry
- 1 large egg
- ½ tsp. of dried oregano
- ¼ tsp. of salt
- ¼ tsp. of pepper
- 24 slices pepperoni

Cooking Instructions:

1. Preheat the oven to 375°F. In a medium bowl, add together the first eight ingredients.
2. Add a pepperoni slice in each of 24 greased mini-muffin cups and fill with the cheese mixture.
3. Bake for 20-25 minutes or until set. Loosen the frittatas by running a knife around sides of muffin cups.
4. Serve warm and enjoy!

Strawberry Coco Smoothie

Preparation Time: 10 minutes

Total Time: 10 minutes

Serves: 4

Ingredients:

- 1 Cup of unsweetened coconut milk
- 2 Tbsp. vanilla extract
- 5 Frozen strawberries
- 4 Tbsp. heavy cream

Cooking Instructions:

1. Put all the ingredients in a blender, and process.
2. Empty into a glass. Top with fresh strawberries.
3. Serve and enjoy!!!

Rosemary Keto Bagels

Preparation Time: 10 minutes

Cook Time: 45 minutes

Total Time: 55 minutes

Serves: 4

Ingredients:

- 1 ½ Cups of almond flour
- ¾ Tsp. baking soda
- ¾ Tsp. xanthan gum
- ¼ Tsp. salt
- 3 Tbsp. psyllium husk powder
- 1 Whole egg
- 3 Egg whites
- ½ Cup of warm water
- 1 Tbsp. rosemary, chopped
- Avocado oil

Cooking Instructions:

1. Preheat oven to 250°F. Combine almond flour, baking soda, xanthan gum and salt together in a bowl.
2. Whisk eggs and warm water together in another bowl. Add psyllium husk. Mix liquid ingredients and dry ingredients.
3. Dredge bagel mould with avocado oil. Put dough into the mould.
4. Spray rosemary on top. Put in oven and bake for about 45 minutes.
5. Remove and set aside to cool before slicing.
6. Serve and enjoy!!!

Strawberry and Black Currant Smoothie

Preparation Time: 10 minutes

Total Time: 10 minutes

Serves: 4

Ingredients:

- ½ Cup of water
- 2 Tbsp. whole or powdered chia seeds
- ½ Tsp. sugar-free vanilla extract
- ½ Cup of fresh blackcurrants
- 3 Fresh strawberries
- 2 Oz. heavy whip cream
- 7 Drops of stevia syrup

Cooking Instructions:

1. Mix all the ingredients in a food processor, and blend.
2. Set aside for about 5 minutes.
3. Empty into a glass.
4. Serve and enjoy!!!

Coconut Macadamia Bars

Preparation Time: 5 minutes

Total Time: 5 minutes

Serves: 6

Calories: 327kcal

Ingredients:

- ½ Cup almond butter
- ¼ Cup coconut oil
- 6 Tbsp. unsweetened shredded coconut
- 60g Macadamia nuts
- 20 Drops Sweet leaf stevia drops

Cooking Instructions:

1. Blend the macadamia nuts a food processor.
2. Mix the almond butter, coconut oil and shredded coconut in a bowl.
3. Put the macadamia nuts and stevia drops in the mixture.
4. Combine and empty the batter into a parchment paper lined baking dish.
5. Put in your freezer overnight and slice.
6. Serve and enjoy!!!

Blueberry Smoothie

Preparation Time: 10 minutes

Total Time: 10 minutes

Serves: 4

Ingredients:

- 1 Tbsp. cold-pressed organic flaxseed oil
- 1 Cup of unsweetened almond
- 1 cup of frozen, unsweetened blueberries

Cooking Instructions:

1. Blend all the above ingredients except the oil in a blender.
2. Empty into a glass.
3. Combine the flax seed oil in it with a spoon.
4. Garnish with blueberries.
5. Serve and enjoy!!!

Buttery Coconut Flour Waffles

Preparation Time: 10 minutes

Cook Time: 20 minutes

Serves: 5

Ingredients:

- 2 Tsp. vanilla extract
- 3 Tbsp. milk full fat
- ½ Cup of butter melted
- 4 Tbsp. coconut flour
- 5 Eggs separate whites from yolks
- 4 Tbsp. granulated stevia
- 1 Tsp. baking powder

Cooking Instructions:

1. Mix the egg yolks, stevia, coconut flour, and baking powder in a bowl.
2. Put the melted butter gently to the flour mixture and combine well.
3. Put the milk and vanilla in the flour and butter mixture and combine together.
4. Whisk the egg whites in another bowl.
5. Softly fold spoons of the egg whites into the flour mixture.
6. Empty mixture into waffle maker and cook for about 20 minutes.
7. Serve and enjoy!!!

Avocado Raspberry Chocolate Smoothie

Preparation Time: 10 minutes

Total Time: 10 minutes

Serves: 4

Ingredients:

- 1/8 Tsp. raspberry extract
- 1 Tbsp. cocoa powder
- Stevia Syrup
- 1 ½ Cups of unsweetened cashew milk
- ½ Avocados
- 1/3 Cup of frozen raspberries

Cooking Instructions:

1. Put all the ingredients in the blender and process. Make a smooth paste.
2. Put Cashew Milk to the mixture.
3. Serve and enjoy!!!

Orange Peel and Ginger Lassi

Preparation Time: 10 minutes

Total Time: 10 minutes

Serves: 4

Ingredients:

- 1 Tsp. freshly grated organic ginger
- Stevia syrup
- 2 Cups of ice-cold water
- 7 Oz. organic full-fat Greek
- 1 Freshly grated orange peel

Cooking Instructions:

1. Put all the ingredients in a blender and process.
2. Put some ice cubes in the glass with the smoothies.
3. Serve and enjoy!!!

Rooibos Tea Latte

Preparation Time: 6 minutes

Cook Time: 6 minutes

Total Time: 12 minutes

Serves: 4

Ingredients:

- 1 Tsp. Brain Octane Oil
- 1 Scoop collagen peptides
- 1 Dropper full CBD oil
- 1 Cup of water
- 2 Bags rooibos tea
- 1 Tbsp. grass-fed butter or ghee

Cooking Instructions:

1. Boil water and put in a mug with both tea bags, and steep for 5 minutes.
2. Remove tea bags and put the remaining ingredients except collagen.
3. Empty mixture into a blender and process.
4. Add collagen and blend with the lowest speed.
5. Serve and enjoy!!!

KETO DIET BRUNCH & DINNER RECIPES

Simple Shrimp Ceviche

Preparation Time: 5 minutes

Total Time: 5 minutes

Serves: 4

Ingredients:

- ½ Cup of sliced red onion
- ½ Cup of chopped tomatoes
- ½ Tsp. salt
- ¼ Tsp. pepper
- Olive oil for drizzling
- 1 Lbs. fresh raw shrimp, cooked, peeled, deveined, and chopped
- 1 Large chopped avocado
- ¼ Cup of roughly chopped fresh cilantro
- 1 Cup of chopped cucumber
- 1/3 Cup of fresh citrus juice from limes

Cooking Instructions:

1. Arrange all your ingredients. Clean, and slice your shrimp into pieces.
2. Put all ingredients in a large bowl and combine together.
3. Serve and enjoy!!!

Baked Pork Chops

Preparation Time: 10 minutes

Cook Time: 1 hour

Total Time: 1 hour 10 minutes

Serves: 4

Ingredients:

- ½ Tsp. onion powder
- ¼ Tsp. chili powder
- ⅛ Tsp. oregano
- 1 Tbsp. avocado oil
- 4 Pork chops
- ½ Cup of grated parmesan cheese
- 1 ½ Tsp. garlic powder
- 1 Tbsp. dried parsley
- 1 Tsp. dried thyme
- 1 Tsp. paprika
- ¾ Tsp. salt
- ½ Tsp. pepper

Cooking Instructions:

1. Preheat oven to 350°F. Spray non-stick cooking spray in a big baking dish. Mix parmesan cheese and spices in small dish and combine together.

2. Over medium heat, place avocado oil in a big skillet. Dredge pork chops in seasoning and put on hot skillet.

3. Brown both sides of pork chops. Remove browned pork chops to the prepared baking dish.

4. Bake pork chops in oven for about 50 minutes. Remove from oven and keep pork chops aside to rest for about 10 minutes.

5. Serve and enjoy!!!

Garlic Parmesan Zucchini Pasta

Preparation Time: 5 minutes

Cook Time: 4 minutes

Total Time: 9 minutes

Serves: 4

Ingredients:

- ½ Cup of chopped tomatoes
- ½ Cup of shredded parmesan cheese
- 1 Cup of fresh basil leaves
- 2 Tsp. lemon juice
- 4 Medium zucchini
- 2 Tbsp. extra virgin olive oil
- 4 Cloves garlic

Cooking Instructions:

1. Put olive oil, garlic, and red pepper flakes in a big skillet. Set to low-medium heat.
2. Once the oil starts boiling around the garlic, put the zucchini noodles. Throw the noodles and cook for about 4 minutes then put off the heat.
3. Put in the tomatoes, lemon juice, parmesan cheese and basil, throw to coat. Make grilled chicken, fish available. Garnish with extra parmesan cheese.
4. Serve and enjoy!!!

Garlic and Herb Pork Loin Roast

Preparation Time: 15 minutes

Cook Time: 75 minutes

Total Time: 1 hour 30 minutes

Serves: 16

Ingredients:

- 3 Lbs. boneless pork loin roast
- 5 Cloves garlic
- 1 Tsp. sea salt or kosher salt
- ½ Tsp. ground black pepper
- 1 Tbsp. Dijon mustard
- 1 Tsp. dried rosemary
- 2 Tsp. garlic powder

Cooking Instructions:

1. Preheat your oven to 375°F. Put pork loin in a baking dish.
2. Combine mustard, salt, garlic powder, pepper, rosemary, and garlic in a bowl.
3. Dredge pork with mixture. Cook pork for about 75 minutes.
4. Serve and enjoy!!!

Chicken and Veggie Shish Kabob

Preparation Time: 10 minutes

Cook Time: 25 minutes

Total Time: 35 minutes

Serves: 4

Ingredients:

- 2 Organic chicken breast, chopped into large chunks
- 2 Large bell peppers, chopped
- ½ Red onion, chopped
- 1 Zucchini, sliced
- ¼ Cup of mushrooms

Marinade for the Chicken:

- ¼ Perfect Keto BBQ Sauce recipe
- 1 Scoop Perfect Keto Unflavored Collagen

Cooking Instructions:

1. Whisk the BBQ sauce and put in the chicken, set to marinate. Slice the vegetables.
2. Divide chicken and vegetables equally onto the skewers. Grill the skewers to 165°F.
3. Serve and enjoy!!!

Chicken Salad with Peach Balsamic Dressing

Preparation Time: 5 minutes

Cook Time: 30 minutes

Total Time: 35 minutes

Serves: 2

Calories: 573 kcal

Ingredients:

- 2 Cups of butter lettuce
- ½ Avocado
- ¼ Cup of red onion, sliced
- ¼ Cup of mozzarella balls
- 3 Tomatoes
- 1 Organic skinless chicken breast
- 3 Pastured hard-boiled eggs, sliced
- 2 Cups of romaine
- Black sesame seeds

Dressing:

- 1 Scoop Perfect Keto Peach Exogenous Ketone Base
- Salt and black pepper to taste
- 2 Tbsp. olive oil
- 1 Tbsp. balsamic vinegar

Cooking Instructions:

1. Preheat the oven to 375ºF. Put the chicken breast and sprinkle with salt and pepper in a baking sheet lined with parchment paper.

2. Bake for about 30 minutes. Divide the lettuces, red onion, mozzarella balls, eggs, tomatoes and chicken equally into two plates.

3. Sprinkle sesame seeds. Combine together the dressing ingredients in a small bowl and empty it over the salad.

4. Serve and enjoy!!!

Midday Boost Latte

Preparation Time: 5 minutes

Total Time: 5 minutes

Serves: 2

Calories: 138 kcal

Ingredients:

- 12 Oz. freshly brewed decaf coffee
- 2 Tbsp. heavy cream or
- Coconut cream
- 1 Scoop Perfect Keto Chocolate Collagen
- 1 Scoop Perfect Keto Chocolate Whey Protein
- ½ Scoop Perfect Keto Nootropic

Cooking Instructions:

1. Put all ingredients in a blender and blend on high speed to combine and become smooth.
2. Serve and enjoy!!!

BBQ Ranch Burgers

Preparation Time: 5 minutes

Cook Time: 5 minutes

Total Time: 10 minutes

Serves: 4

Calories: 170 kcal

Ingredients:

- 1 Lbs. ground turkey
- 1 Tbsp. no sugar added ketchup
- 1 Tbsp. Trader Joe's BBQ coffee seasoning mix
- ¼ Tsp. liquid smoke
- 1 Tsp. worcestershire sauce
- 1 Tbsp. dried minced onion
- 1 Tsp. garlic powder
- 1 Tsp. dried parsley
- ½ Tsp. onion powder
- ½ Tsp. dried dill
- 1 Tsp. sea salt
- ¼ Tsp. black pepper

Cooking Instructions:

1. Put ground turkey, ketchup, and all seasonings in a big bowl. Use your hands to combine well.
2. Separate patties into 4 burgers. Cook on the BBQ pan for about 4 minutes on both sides. Gather burgers.
3. Serve and enjoy!!!

Crack Slaw

Preparation Time: 10 minutes

Cook Time: 10 minutes

Total Time: 20 minutes

Serves: 4

Calories: 212 kcal

Ingredients:

- 1 Tbsp. sesame oil
- 1 Tsp. coconut amino
- 1 Tsp. ground ginger
- ⅛ Tsp. black pepper
- ⅛ Tsp. salt
- 2 Stalks green onion, roughly chopped
- 1 ½ Tsp. sesame seeds
- 1 Lbs. cabbage, roughly chopped
- 1 Lbs. ground pork
- 2 tbsp. chicken broth
- 1 Tbsp. minced garlic

Cooking Instructions:

1. Blend chopped cabbage in food processor and keep aside. Brown and crush ground meat over medium heat in a large skillet.
2. In a small bowl, mix together chicken broth, sesame oil, coconut amino, ground ginger, minced garlic, pepper, and salt.
3. Empty into pan of ground pork and stir. Put cabbage in the pan and toss with tongs. Cook for about 5 minutes. Take from heat, flip to serving bowls.
4. Garnish with green onion and sesame seeds. Serve and enjoy!!!

Shrimp Stir Fry with Baked Cauliflower Rice

Preparation Time: 8 minutes

Cook Time: 15 minutes

Total Time: 23 minutes

Serves: 4

Calories: 357 kcal

Ingredients:

- 4 Baby bella mushrooms
- 1 Inch piece of lemon rind
- 2 Tsp. pink Himalayan salt, more to taste
- 3 Tbsp. bacon fat
- 12 Oz. frozen riced cauliflower
- 2 Tbsp. MCT oil
- 16 Oz. shrimp
- 2 Inch nub of ginger root
- 4 Stalks green onion
- 2 Garlic cloves

Cooking Instructions:

1. Preheat your oven to 400°F. Put your cauliflower rice on a sheet pan, sprinkle with MCT oil and drizzle with pink Himalayan salt.

2. Put in the oven and bake for about 10 minutes. Slice your peeled ginger root and garlic cloves. Slice your green onion into pieces. Skin a slice of lemon rind off.

3. Put a large skillet on medium heat. Put the bacon fat and all your aromatics and cook. Put the shrimp and cook, stir often.

4. Put the coconut amino and salt, stir for another 3 minutes. Garnish with more green onion, sesame seeds and chili flakes. Serve and enjoy!!!

Mushroom Bacon Skillet

Preparation Time: 10 minutes

Cook Time: 10 minutes

Total Time: 20 minutes

Serves: 2

Ingredients:

- ½ Tsp salt
- 2 Sprigs thyme
- 1 Tbsp. garlic confit
- 4 Slices pastured pork bacon
- 2 Cups of halved mushrooms

Cooking Instructions:

1. Heat a large skillet over medium heat. Prepare your ingredient. Chop the bacon into pieces. Cut the mushrooms in half
2. Separate the thyme leaves from the stems. Put the bacon in the skillet and cook each side and put the mushrooms. Cook and stir regularly.
3. Put the salt, thyme and garlic, continue cooking and stirring for another 5 minutes. Top over greens, with boiled eggs.
4. Serve and enjoy!!!

Curry Chicken Lettuce Wraps

Preparation Time: 5 minutes

Cook Time: 15 minutes

Total Time: 20 minutes

Serves: 2

Calories: 554 kcal

Ingredients:

- 1 Tsp. black pepper
- 3 Tbsp. ghee
- 1 Cup of cauliflower rice
- 8 Small lettuce leaves
- ¼ Cup of Lactose free sour cream
- 1 Lbs. boneless skinless chicken thighs
- ¼ Cup of minced onion
- 2 Garlic cloves, minced
- 2 Tsp. Curry Powder
- 1Tsp. pink Himalayan salt

Cooking Instructions:

1. Arrange your vegetables and keep aside. Slice your chicken thighs into pieces. Put a large skillet on medium heat. Put in 2 Tbsp. of ghee and add onion and stir.

2. Put in the chicken, garlic and salt and mix well. Cook the chicken, stir often for about 8 minutes. Put in 1 Tbsp. of ghee, the curry and the cauliflower rice and cook.

3. Spoon the curry chicken mixture into each of your lettuce leave. Top with a spoonful of cream. Serve and enjoy!!!

Roasted Chicken Stacks

Preparation Time: 10 minutes

Cook Time: 40 minutes

Total Time: 50 minutes

Serves: 5

Calories: 369 kcal

Ingredients:

- 1 Tsp. black pepper
- 2 Tsp. Italian herb blend
- ½ Cup of bone broth
- ¼ Cup of avocado oil
- 5 Small chicken breasts
- 1 Head of savoy cabbage
- 5 Slices of prosciutto
- 3 Tbsp. coconut flour
- 2 Tsp. salt, more to taste

Cooking Instructions:

1. Pre-heat oven to 400°F. Mix the chicken breast, salt, pepper, herbs and coconut flour in a plastic bag and toss to dredge the chicken.
2. Sprinkle a tbsp. of the oil on the pan. Mince the savoy cabbage and make 5 small piles of minced cabbage on the sheet pan.
3. Add a little salt and sprinkle a little oil on them. Put a dredge chicken breast over each one. Top each chicken piece with a slice of prosciutto.
4. Sprinkle with remaining oil. Bake at 400°F for about 30 minutes. Empty the broth into the sheet pan. Bake for another 10 minutes. Remove from the oven.
5. Serve and enjoy!!!

Keto Chili

Preparation Time: 5 minutes

Cook Time: 30 minutes

Total Time: 35 minutes

Serves: 6

Calories: 359 kcal

Ingredients:

- 2 Tsp. garlic powder
- 1 Tbsp. cumin
- 1 Tsp. salt
- 1 Tsp. black pepper
- 1 15 Oz. can no-salt-added tomato sauce
- 1 16.2 Oz. container Kettle & Fire Beef Bone Broth
- ½ Tbsp. avocado oil
- 2 Ribs celery, chopped
- 2 Lbs. ground beef
- 1 Tsp. ground chipotle chili powder
- 1 Tbsp. chili powder

Cooking Instructions:

1. Put avocado oil over medium heat in a large pot. Put chopped celery and cook for about 4 minutes. Flip celery to another bowl and keep aside.
2. In same pot, put beef and spices, cook the beef. Reduce heat to medium-low, put tomato sauce and beef bone broth in the cooked beef.
3. Cook while covered for 10 minutes, stirring irregularly. Put celery back to pot and mix. Serve and enjoy!!!

Lemon Herb Meatloaf

Prep Time: 10 minutes

Cook Time: 50 minutes

Total Time: 1 hour

Serves: 6

Calories: 344 kcal

Ingredients:

- 2 Lbs. lean grass fed ground beef
- ½ Tbsp. fine Himalayan salt
- 1 Tsp. black pepper
- ¼ Cup of Nutritional Yeast
- 2 Large eggs
- 2 Tbsp. avocado oil
- 1 Tbsp. lemon zest
- ¼ Cup of chopped parsley
- ¼ Cup of chopped fresh oregano
- 4 Cloves garlic

Cooking Instructions:

1. Preheat oven to 400°F. Mix the ground beef, salt, black pepper and nutritional yeast in a large bowl.
2. Mix the eggs, oil, herbs and garlic in a blender and blend well to mix and mince. Put the egg mixture in the beef and combine.
3. Place the beef in a small loaf pan. Smooth and flatten out. Cook in the oven center rack for about 60 minutes.
4. Gently take from the oven and roll the pan over the sink to drain the liquid. Allow to cool for 10 minutes before slicing into sizes. Garnish with lemon. Serve and enjoy!!!

White Turkey Chili

Preparation Time: 5 minutes

Cook Time: 15 minutes

Total Time: 20 minutes

Calories: 388 kcal

Serves: 5

Ingredients:

- 1 Tbsp. Mustard
- 1 Tsp. of salt, black pepper, thyme, celery salt, garlic powder
- 1 Lbs. Organic ground turkey
- 2 Cups riced cauliflower
- 2 Garlic cloves
- 2 Cups full fat coconut milk
- 2 Tbsp. coconut oil
- ½ Vidalia onion

Cooking Instructions:

1. Heat the coconut oil in a big pot. Put shred onion and garlic into the hot oil. Mix for about 3 minutes and put the ground turkey.
2. Divide with the spatula and stir constantly. Put the seasoning mix, rice cauliflower and mix well.
3. Put the coconut milk, bring to a boil and reduce for 8 minutes, stir regularly. Combine in shredded cheese for an extra thick sauce.
4. Serve and enjoy!!!

Loaded Cauliflower Bake

Preparation Time: 15 minutes

Cook Time: 45 minutes

Total Time: 1 hour

Serves: 4

Calories: 498 kcal

Ingredients:

- 1 ¼ Cup of shredded sharp cheddar cheese, separated
- Salt and pepper to taste
- 6 Slices bacon, cooked and crumbled
- ¼ Cup of chopped green onions
- 1 Large head cauliflower, cut into florets
- 2 Tbsp. butter
- 1 Cup of heavy cream
- 2 Oz. cream cheese

Cooking Instructions:

1. Preheat oven to 350°F. In a big pot of boiling water, cook cauliflower florets for about 2 minutes and drain cauliflower.
2. Melt together butter, heavy cream, shredded cheddar cheese, cream cheese, salt, and pepper in a medium pot and combine.
3. Put cauliflower florets, cheese sauce, crumbled bacon, and green onions in a baking dish and mix together.
4. Top with remaining shredded cheddar cheese, crumbled bacon, and green onions. Bake for about 30 minutes.
5. Serve and enjoy!!!

KETO DIET POULTRY RECIPES

Grilled Chicken Caesar Salad

Preparation Time: 10 minutes

Total Time: 10 minutes

Serves: 4

Calories: 372 kcal

Ingredients:

- ½ Cup of shredded Parmesan cheese
- Freshly ground pepper
- 1 Lb. romaine lettuce
- 12 Oz. Garlic Herbed Grilled Chicken
- ¾ Cup of Lemony Caesar Dressing

Lemony Caesar Dressing:

- 2 Tbsp. fresh lemon juice or more
- Zest of one lemon
- ¼ Cup of grated Parmesan cheese
- 1 Cup of mayo
- 1 ½ Tsp. anchovy paste
- 1 Clove medium garlic
- ¼ Tsp. salt
- 1 ½ Tsp. Dijon mustard
- 1 ½ Tsp. Worcestershire sauce

Cooking Instructions:

1. Put the chicken, romaine, and 1 cup of Lemony Caesar Dressing in a large mixing bowl. Using your hands, give it a good mix.

2. Flip the dressed salad onto a serving plate and top with shredded Parmesan cheese and freshly ground black pepper.

3. Serve and enjoy!!!

Caprese Chicken Mozzarella

Preparation Time: 5 minutes

Cook Time: 15 minutes

Total Time: 20 minutes

Serves: 4

Calories: 402 kcal

Ingredients:

- 1 Cup of commercially prepared marinara sauce
- 4 Oz. fresh mozzarella cheese sliced
- Basil
- 4 Boneless skinless chicken breasts
- 1 Tbsp. olive oil
- 3 Tsp. Garlic Herb Seasoning Blend
- Salt
- 2 Tbsp. olive oil

Cooking Instructions:

1. Preheat your skillet on a medium heat. Brush the chicken breast with the olive oil alongside with salt and spray the Garlic Herb Seasoning Blend on top.
2. Sauté the chicken in the skillet with plenty oil. Put the chicken in the cooking shit and cook for about 5 minutes. Turn it over and cook for another 5 minutes.
3. Pour ¼ cup of sauce on top of the chicken and put 1 Oz. of the sliced fresh mozzarella cheese.
4. Close the shit with a lid and cook for about 2 minutes. Top with basil.
5. Serve and enjoy!!!

BBQ Chicken Crust Pizza

Preparation Time: 15 minutes

Cook Time: 25 minutes

Total Time: 40 minutes

Serves: 4

Calories: 355 kcal

Ingredients:

- ¼ Cup of sliced red onion
- 2 Slices crisp bacon, crumbled
- Chopped cilantro
- 1 Lb. shredded rotisserie chicken
- 1 Cup Part-Skim Grated Mozzarella Cheese
- 2 Large eggs
- ¼ Cup of Sugar-free BBQ sauce
- 1 ½ Cups of smoked Gouda cheese, grated

Cooking Instructions:

1. Cut the chicken into chunks sizes. Put into a food processor to chop and put salt and pepper.
2. Preheat the oven to 400º F. Place parchment paper on a baking sheet and give it a good stir.
3. Pat the chicken on the parchment and be sure you leave no holes. Bake for about 20 minutes.
4. Sprinkle the BBQ sauce on the crust, top with onions, Gouda cheese, and bacon and bake for another 10 minutes. Top with cilantro.
5. Serve and enjoy!!!

Chicken Schnitzel a La Holstein

Preparation Time: 10 minutes

Cook Time: 10 minutes

Total Time: 20 minutes

Serves: 2

Calories: 672 kcal

Ingredients:

- Pepper
- 1 Tbsp. olive oil
- 2 Tbsp. unsalted butter
- Fresh flat-leaf parsley, chopped
- 2 Chicken breasts
- ½ Cup of almond flour
- ¼ Cup of Bob's Red Mill Golden Flax Meal
- 3 Large eggs
- Salt

Cooking Instructions:

1. In a medium mixing bowl, combine together the flaxseed meal and almond flour. Break the egg into another mixing bowl.
2. Burry the chicken breast in the bowl containing the egg and burry it finally in the bowl containing the almond mixture. Put salt and pepper.
3. Preheat olive oil in the skillet. On a medium heat, cook the chicken for about 10 minutes. Flip over during half way of cooking time.
4. Fry the eggs to your consistency and flip the chicken onto 2 serving plates. Place one egg beside each chicken and top with parsley.
5. Serve and enjoy!!!

Buffalo Chicken Dip

Preparation Time: 10 minutes

Cook Time: 10 minutes

Total Time: 20 minutes

Serves: 12

Calories: 183 kcal

Ingredients:

- 2 Tbsp. chopped green onions
- 2 Tbsp. chopped green onions
- 1/3 Cup of blue cheese crumbles
- 3 Cups of shredded chicken
- 8 Oz. cream cheese, sliced
- 1 Cup of shredded mozzarella cheese
- 1/3 Cup of Franks Buffalo Sauce
- ½ Cup of creamy Ranch salad dressing

Cooking Time:

1. On a low heat on a frying pan, put the mozzarella and cream cheese and melt. Put the shredded chicken and Buffalo sauce.
2. Put the green onions, and ranch dressing. Give it a good stir. Heat the mixture for sometimes and flip onto a serving plate.
3. Top with scallions and blue cheese.
4. Serve and enjoy!!!

Homemade Sloppy Joes

Preparation Time: 5 minutes

Cook Time: 25 minutes

Total Time: 30 minutes

Serves: 4

Calories: 233 kcal

Ingredients:

- 2 Tsp. Worcestershire sauce
- 1 Cup of beef broth
- ¼ Tsp. salt
- 1 Lb. lean ground beef
- ½ Cup of diced green bell pepper
- ¼ Cup of diced onion
- 1 Clove garlic minced
- ¼ Cup of tomato paste
- 2 Tbsp. Sukrin Gold
- 1 Tbsp. yellow mustard
- 2 Tsp. red wine vinegar
- Pepper

Cooking instructions:

1. In a medium frying pan, put the ground beef, cut the meat into small pieces and cook on a medium heat for about 7 minutes.
2. Check when the meat is about to be well cooked, put the remaining ingredients and put water.
3. Simmer on a medium low heat, reduce the heat and simmer uncovered for 15 minutes. Serve and enjoy!!!

Mexican Chicken Casserole

Preparation Time: 20 minutes

Cook Time: 35 minutes

Total Time: 55 minutes

Serves: 8

Calories: 184 kcal

Ingredients:

- Extra enchilada sauce
- Sour cream
- Diced tomatoes
- Diced avocado
- Fresh cilantro
- 6 Cups cooked cauliflower rice
- 2 Cups finely shredded Mexican Blend Cheese
- 1 Large egg
- 4 Oz. diced green chilies
- 1 Tsp. ground cumin
- ¼ Tsp. salt
- 2 Cups of shredded cooked chicken
- 1 ¼ Cups of enchilada sauce

Cooking Instructions:

1. Preheat oven to 400°F. Put coconut oil in the casserole pan and shred the chicken with two forks.

2. Mix together ¾ cup of the shredded cheese, cauliflower rice, egg, green chilies, cumin and salt in a large mixing bowl.

3. Put the cauliflower rice mixture into the casserole pan and bake for about 25 minutes.

4. Mix together the shredded meat and enchilada sauce in a medium mixing bowl. Pour on top of the baked cauliflower rice mixture.

5. Put the remaining 1 ¾ cups shredded cheese and take back the baking pan to the oven and bake for about 10 minutes.

6. Serve and enjoy!!!

Chicken Enchilada Dip

Preparation Time: 10 minutes

Cook Time: 1 hour

Total Time: 1 hour 10 minutes

Serves: 6

Calories: 276 kcal

Ingredients:

- ½ Tsp. granulated onion
- ¼ Tsp. salt
- 2 Tbsp. sliced green onions
- 2 Tbsp. fresh cilantro, minced
- 2 Cups of shredded rotisserie chicken
- 2 Cups of shredded Monterey Jack cheese
- 4 Oz. cream cheese
- 4 Oz. diced green chilies
- 1 Can water
- 1 ½ Tsp. ground cumin
- ¾ Tsp. white pepper
- ½ Tsp. granulated garlic

Cooking Instructions:

1. For the enchilada dip, put all the ingredients into a small crock-pot.
2. Cook for about 60 minutes. Give it a good stir. Flip onto a serving plate.
3. Serve and enjoy!!!

Chicken Pizza Crust

Preparation Time: 10 minutes

Cook Time: 30 minutes

Total Time: 40 minutes

Serves: 4

Calories: 276 kcal

Ingredients:

- 2 Large eggs
- Salt
- 1 Lb. shredded chicken breast
- 1 Cup pre-shredded mozzarella cheese
- Pepper

Cooking Instructions:

1. Slice the chicken into chunks. Put into a food blender to chop and season with salt and pepper.
2. Preheat the oven to 400° F. Place parchment paper on a baking sheet and give it a good stir. Pat the chicken on the parchment without leaving holes.
3. Bake for about 20 minutes, top with your favorite pizza toppings and bake for another 10 minutes.
4. Serve and enjoy!!!

Spinach Strawberry Pecan Salad

Preparation Time: 10 minutes

Cook Time: 15 minutes

Total Time: 25 minutes

Serves: 2

Calories: 524 kcal

Ingredients:

Salad:

- 1 Oz. pecans
- 1 Oz. crumbled feta cheese
- 2 Tbsp. red onion, sliced
- 6 Oz. baby spinach
- 4 Oz. grilled chicken, sliced
- 3 Oz. strawberries, sliced

Vinaigrette Dressing:

- ½ Tsp. sweetener
- ⅛ Tsp. dried thyme
- 1 Pinch of salt
- ¼ Cup of light olive oil
- 1 Tbsp. balsamic vinegar
- 1 Tbsp. red wine vinegar
- 1 Tbsp. water
- 2 Tsp. minced red onion
- 1 Pinch of Pepper

Cooking Instructions:

1. Combine together the dressing and keep aside. Cut the strawberries, chicken, and onions.

2. In 2 bowls, put the ingredients in layers and put the dressing on the top.

3. Serve and enjoy!!!

Smoked Chicken Leg Quarters

Preparation Time: 10 minutes

Cook Time: 2 hours

Total Time: 2 hours 10 minutes

Serves: 4

Calories: 261 kcal

Ingredients:

- Salt
- Signature blend (apple wood or pecan)
- 4 Chicken leg quarters
- 3 Tsp. Dry Rub
- 1 Tbsp. olive oil

Cooking Instruction:

1. With a paper towel, pat dry chicken leg quarters and remove the fat on the chicken if any.
2. Brush oil on the chicken and spray the surface with the dry rub. Keep it for about 20 minutes.
3. Switch grill to smoke and allow it to heat for about 15 minutes. Keep the chicken skin side up and smoke for about an hour.
4. Cook at 350°F for about 60 minutes.
5. Serve and enjoy!!!

Tangy Ranch Chicken Wings

Preparation Time: 10 minutes

Cook Time: 50 minutes

Total Time: 1 hour

Serves: 4

Calories: 341 kcal

Ingredients:

- 2 ½ Tsp. Homemade Ranch Seasoning
- ¼ Tsp. Salt
- Olive oil spray
- 2 Lbs. Chicken wing pieces
- 2 Tsp. olive oil
- 2 Tsp. baking powder

Cooking Instructions:

1. Preheat oven to 375° F. Pat dry the chicken wings with paper towels and place in a large mixing bowl.
2. Combine together the chicken wings, 2 Tsp. olive oil, and 1 Tsp. baking powder. Give it a good stir.
3. Keep the chicken wings on a wire rack on a large baking pan. Bake for about 40 minutes. Flip over half way on the cooking time.
4. Get the chicken out from the oven, Keep under the broiler for about 10 minutes. Flip the chicken onto a large bowl and sprinkle olive oil.
5. Pour 1 Tsp. ranch seasoning on top of the chicken and give it a good mix. Do this step again and put ¼ Tsp. salt along with the seasoning.
6. Serve and enjoy!!!

Chicken Cordon Bleu Casserole

Preparation Time: 15 minutes

Cook Time: 30 minutes

Total Time: 45 minutes

Serves: 8

Calories: 452 kcal

Ingredients:

- 1 Oz. lemon juice
- ½ Tsp. salt
- 5 Oz. Swiss cheese
- 6 Cups of shredded cooked chicken
- 6 Oz. ham sliced
- 4 Oz. butter melted
- 6 Oz. cream cheese softened
- 1 Tbsp. Dijon mustard

Cooking Instructions:

1. Preheat the oven to 350°F. Place the chicken into baking pan and spread pieces of ham on top.
2. Mix together the softened cream cheese, melted butter, mustard, lemon juice, and salt in a large mixing bowl with an electric mixer. Give it a good blend.
3. Sprinkle the sauce on top of the chicken and ham in the baking dish. Place the slices of Swiss cheese on top of the sauce.
4. Bake for about 40 minutes.
5. Serve and enjoy!!!

Chicken Tenders

Preparation Time: 10 minutes

Cook Time: 25 minutes

Total Time: 35 minutes

Serves: 2

Calories: 587 kcal

Ingredients:

- 2 Eggs beaten
- 1 Lb. chicken tenderloin
- Low carb ketchup
- ½ Cup of almond flour
- ¼ Cup of flaxseed meal
- ¼ Tsp. paprika
- Salt
- Pepper

Cooking Instructions:

1. Preheat the oven to 375ºF. Mix together almond flour, flaxseed meal, paprika, salt and pepper in a medium mixing bowl.
2. Put the eggs into another bowl. Burry a chicken tenderloin into the egg mixture and then dip it into the dry mixture.
3. On a baking pan lined with wire rack, place the chicken. Do this for the remaining tenderloins.
4. Bake for 25 minutes and top with low carb ketchup.
5. Serve and enjoy!!!

Chicken Alfredo Casserole with Broccoli

Preparation Time: 15 minutes

Cook Time: 50 minutes

Total Time: 1 hour 5 minutes

Serves: 20

Calories: 549 kcal

Ingredients:

- 32 Oz. broccoli chopped
- 32 Oz. cauliflower chopped
- 16 Oz. mozzarella sliced
- 3 ½ Lbs. chicken breast skinless and boneless
- Kosher salt
- 6 Tbsp. olive oil extra virgin
- 6 Cloves garlic minced
- 6 Cups of heavy cream
- ½ Tsp. white pepper
- 16 Oz. mozzarella chopped
- Black pepper
- 3 Tbsp. olive oil extra virgin
- 6 Tbsp. butter
- ¾ Cup of parmesan cheese grated
- ¼ Cup of dried parsley

Cooking Instructions:

1. Add salt and pepper to chicken and fry with an olive oil. Shred the chicken with two forks.

2. Melt butter and olive oil in medium saucepan using medium low heat. Put the pepper, garlic cream and then simmer the mixture.

3. Put the Parmesan cheese and mozzarella. Stir constantly and remove from heat when you are satisfied with the thickness.

4. Mix together the cauliflower, broccoli, and diced chicken in casserole pan.

5. Put the source on the chicken vegetable mixture and mix properly.

6. Top with sliced mozzarella and bake at 350°F for about 55 minutes.

7. Serve and enjoy!!!

Chicken Tikka Masala

Preparation Time: 10 minutes

Cook Time: 2 minutes

Total Time: 12 minutes

Serves: 6

Ingredients:

- 1 Tsp. salt
- ½ Tsp. freshly ground pepper
- ½ Cup of fresh cilantro, chopped
- 1 Yellow onion, peeled and chopped
- 1 Tbsp. butter
- Pepper
- 2 Tsp. coriander
- 2 Tsp. cumin
- 1 ½ Tsp. paprika
- ½ Tsp. cardamom
- ½ Tsp. cayenne pepper
- ¼ Tsp. nutmeg
- 1 Tbsp. fresh ginger, minced
- ¼ Cup of tomato paste
- 1 Cup of cream
- 2 Chicken breasts, cut
- Sea Salt

Cooking Instructions:

1. Preheat a skillet. Put butter and sauté. Put the onions and cook to your desired consistency. Put chicken, salt and pepper.

2. Cook both sides of the chicken on a medium low heat. Put cumin, coriander, paprika, cardamom, cayenne pepper and nutmeg. Cook for about 2 minutes.

3. Put tomato paste, fresh ginger, and cream to the skillet. Give it a good mix. Increase heat to medium and simmer the mixture.

4. Reduce the heat and continue cooking. Keep on stirring continuously. Put salt, pepper, and cilantro. Serve and enjoy!!!

Chicken Bacon Ranch Casserole

Preparation Time: 5 minutes

Cook Time: 15 minutes

Total Time: 20 minutes

Serves: 8

Ingredients:

- 1 Cup of Mozzarella cheese, shredded
- 1 Cup of Cheddar cheese, shredded
- 1 Lb. Frozen spinach, thawed and squeezed
- 2 Lb. Chicken breast, cooked and shredded
- 8 Slices Bacon, cooked and sliced
- 3 Cloves Garlic, minced
- ¾ Cup of Ranch dressing

Cooking Instructions:

1. Preheat the oven to 375ºF. In a large mixing bowl, mix together the bacon, chicken, spinach, garlic, ranch dressing, and half of the shredded cheeses.
2. Give it a good mix and flip onto a stoneware casserole dish. Top with remaining cheddar cheeses and shredded mozzarella.
3. Bake for about 15 minutes.
4. Serve and enjoy!!!

Caprese Hassel-back Chicken

Preparation Time: 10 minutes

Cook Time: 25 minutes

Total Time: 35 minutes

Serves: 4

Calories 365kcal

Ingredients:

- 2 Tbsp. olive oil
- 2 Tbsp. balsamic vinegar
- Sea salt
- 4 Large chicken breasts
- 4 Oz. fresh mozzarella cheese
- 2 Medium roma tomatoes, sliced
- ¼ Cup of fresh basil, cut
- Pepper

Cooking Instructions:

1. Preheat the oven to 400° F. Place parchment paper on a baking pan. Make about 6 deep slits in each chicken breast but do not cut it out.
2. Season both sides of the chicken with black pepper and sea salt. Put the chicken on the baking sheet.
3. Thinly cut the tomatoes and mozzarella and cut the pieces again to a size wider than the thickness of your chicken breast.
4. In each of the slits in the chicken, stuff a tomato slice, mozzarella, and a whole basil leaf. prinkle the chicken with olive oil and balsamic vinegar.
5. Bake for about 25 minutes. Spray the remaining fresh basil ribbons on top when the chicken is well cooked.
6. Serve and enjoy!!!

KETO DIET SOUP, STEW & SALAD RECIPES

Keto Chicken and Cabbage Stew

Preparation Time: 10 minutes

Cook Time: 1 hour

Total Time: 1 hour 10 minutes

Serves: 4

Ingredients:

- ½ Cabbage, sliced
- 3 Cups of water
- Salt
- 3 Tbsp. coconut oil
- 2 Chicken breasts, diced
- 4 Slices bacon, diced
- ½ Onion, diced
- Pepper

Cooking Instructions:

1. Put coconut oil in your skillet and sauté the bacon, chicken, and onion to your desired consistency.
2. Put water and cabbage and bring it to a boil. Lock the lid and cook on low heat for 1 hour. Season with salt and pepper.
3. Serve and enjoy!!!

Southern Potlikker Soup

Preparation Time: 10 minutes

Cook Time: 1 hour 30 minutes

Total Time: 1 hour 40 minutes

Serves: 6

Ingredients:

- 1 Tbsp. apple cider vinegar
- 1 Tbsp. Sriracha
- Sea salt
- 3 Tbsp. ghee
- 1 Large onion, diced
- 2 Carrots, peeled and chopped
- 6 Cups chicken
- 4 Cups chopped kale
- 6 Cups chopped collards
- Ground Pepper
- 1 Lb. uncured, fully-cooked ham steak
- 3 Garlic cloves, minced
- 2 Celery stalks, chopped

Cooking Instructions:

1. Heat butter in a deep pot, put ham, onion, garlic, celery, and carrots. Cook and stir continuously.
2. Put broth, apple cider vinegar, greens, Sriracha and bring to a boil. Close the pot, lower the heat and simmer for about 1 hour 30 minutes.
3. Season with salt and pepper. Serve and enjoy!!!

Thai Tom Sap Pork Ribs Soup

Preparation Time: 5 minutes

Cook Time: 2 hours

Total Time: 2 hour 5 minutes

Serves: 4

Ingredients:

- Juice from 1 lime
- 2 Tbsp. fish sauce
- Salt
- 1 Lb. pork spare ribs
- 2 Small red shallots, chopped
- 4 Small lemongrass stalks, chopped
- 10 Thick slices of galangal
- 8 Cups of water
- 10 Kaffir lime leaves, sliced

Cooking Instructions:

1. Put the water into a large pot, put the pork spare ribs and bring to a boil for about 10 minutes. Drain the water out.
2. Put a fresh 8 cups of water in the large pot along with the ribs, lemongrass, shallots, salt and galangal.
3. Close the lid and allow it to simmer on low heat for about an hour. Put the kaffir lime leaves, juice from 1 lime, fish sauce, and salt.
4. Serve and enjoy!!!

Egg Drop Soup

Preparation Time: 5 minutes

Cook Time: 10 minutes

Total Time: 15 minutes

Serves: 2

Ingredients:

- 3 Medium eggs
- 4 Green onions sliced
- 3 ½ Cups of chicken broth
- 2 Tsp. gluten-free tamari sauce
- 1 Thumb-sized piece of fresh ginger, peeled and sliced

Cooking Instructions:

1. On a stove-top, put the chicken broth in a cooking pan alongside with tamari and ginger. Allow it to simmer for about 3 minutes on low heat.
2. Separate the stock into a clean pan. Place on a low heat. Beat the egg into a separate small mixing bowl.
3. Get the cooking pan of the broth out from the heat and sprinkle the eggs into the broth and give it a good mix.
4. Top with sliced green onions.
5. Serve and enjoy!!!

One-Pot Beef Stew

Preparation Time: 10 minutes

Cook Time: 1 hour 15 minutes

Total Time: 1 hour 25 minutes

Serves: 4

Ingredients:

- 2 Sprigs of thyme, whole
- 4 Bay leaves
- Salt
- 2 Tbsp. avocado oil
- 2 Cups of water
- 1 Lb. beef stew meat
- 4 Slices of bacon, diced
- 1 Onion, diced
- 2 Stalks of celery, chopped
- 1 Carrot, peeled and chopped
- Pepper

Cooking Instructions:

1. In a large pot, put avocado oil and sauté both beef and bacon using high heat. Put the onion and continue sautéing for some times.

2. Put water and bring the mixture to a boil. Put the carrot, celery, thyme, bay leaves, and salt. Close the lid and allow it to simmer for about 1 hour.

3. After this time, remove the bay leaves and thyme stalks. Top with remaining thyme leaves.

4. Serve and enjoy!!!

Asian Chicken Meatball Soup

Preparation Time: 20 minutes

Cook Time: 15 minutes

Total Time: 35 minutes

Serves: 2

Ingredients:

For the chicken meatballs:

- 1 Tbsp. of fresh ginger, minced
- Salt
- 0.6 Lb. of ground chicken
- 1 Tbsp. of chives, chopped
- Pepper
- 2 Tbsp. of avocado oil

For the broth:

- 2 Green onions, sliced
- 5 Slices of fresh ginger
- 2 ½ Cups of chicken broth
- 2 Star anise
- 1 Tsp. of fish sauce

Cooking Instructions:

1. Mix together the chives, ground chicken, ginger, salt and pepper. Make into a small ping-pong sized balls and refrigerate while you prepare the fragrant broth.

2. Spread the chicken broth into a cooking pan alongside with the fish sauce, star anise, and ginger. Boil, lower the heat and simmer for about 15 minutes.

3. Heat olive oil in a cooking pan and cook the chicken meatballs to your desired consistency. Taste for flavor and put more if necessary.

4. Strain and slice between two bowls. Put the cooked meatballs into the bowls containing broth and top with green onions.

5. Serve and enjoy!!!

Chicken Cobb Salad with Cobb Salad Dressing

Preparation Time: 20 minutes

Total Time: 20 minutes

Serves: 2

Calories: 632 kcal

Ingredients:

- ½ Hass avocado, cubed
- 3 Green onions, sliced
- 6 Tbsp. Cobb Salad Dressing
- 180G Romaine lettuce, chopped
- 2 Large hard boiled eggs, sliced
- 2 Oz. cheddar cheese, cubed
- 4 Oz. cooked chicken breast, diced
- 4 Slices cooked bacon, crumbled

Cooking Instructions:

1. Mix together the Cobb salad dressing and romaine lettuce.
2. Share the mixture into 2 serving plates.
3. Serve and enjoy!!!

Spinach Strawberry Pecan Salad

Preparation Time: 10 minutes

Cook Time: 15 minutes

Total Time: 25 minutes

Serves: 2

Calories: 524 kcal

Ingredients:

Salad:

- 1 Oz. pecans
- 1 Oz. crumbled feta cheese
- 2 Tbsp. red onion, sliced
- 6 Oz. baby spinach
- 4 Oz. grilled chicken, sliced
- 3 Oz. strawberries, sliced

Vinaigrette Dressing:

- 2 Tsp. minced red onion
- ½ Tsp. sweetener
- 1/8 Tsp. dried thyme
- 1 Pinch each salt
- ¼ Cup of light olive oil
- 1 Tbsp. balsamic vinegar
- 1 Tbsp. red wine vinegar
- 1 Tbsp. water
- Pepper

Cooking Instructions:

1. Combine the dressing ingredients and keep aside.
2. Cut the strawberries, chicken, and onions.
3. Share the mixture into 2 bowls and spread the dressing on top.
4. Serve and enjoy!!!

Greek Salad

Preparation Time: 15 minutes

Total Time: 15 minutes

Serves: 4

Calories: 353 kcal

Ingredients:

Salad:

- 2 Oz. feta cheese, crumbled
- 20 Kalamata Olives
- 1 Oz. red onion, sliced
- 12 Oz. Romaine Lettuce, chopped
- 1 Medium tomato, cut into wedges
- 4 Oz. cucumber, sliced

Greek Vinaigrette Dressing:

- ½ Tsp. dried oregano, rubbed
- ¼ Tsp. dried marjoram, rubbed
- ¼ Tsp. salt
- ½ Cup of olive oil
- ¼ Cup of lemon juice
- 2 Tbsp. water
- 1 Tbsp. minced shallot
- ½ Tsp. garlic, grated
- 1/8 Tsp. pepper
- 2 Tsp. Sukrin

Cooking Instructions:

1. In a medium jar, combine together all the dressing ingredients. Give it a good mix. Give the lettuce a good wash, slice and put in a serving plate.

2. Cut the tomato, cucumber, and onion. Place them equally on the lettuce. Top with salad ingredients that remain.

3. Serve and enjoy!!!

Sweet Bell Pepper Salad

Preparation Time: 15 minutes

Total Time: 15 minutes

Serves: 6

Calories: 112 kcal

Ingredients:

- 2 Oz. feta cheese crumbled
- ½ Tsp garlic, minced
- 1 Lb. mixed bell peppers, sliced
- 1 Fennel bulb, sliced
- 2 Oz. onion, sliced

Dressing:

- ½ Tsp. Fines Herbs
- ¼ Tsp. salt
- 3 Tbsp. extra virgin olive oil
- 2 Tbsp. Champagne vinegar
- 1 Pinch pepper

Cooking Instructions:

1. Cut all the vegetables and put them into a large mixing bowl. Prepare the dressing by combining the ingredients together.
2. Give it a good mix, taste and put more seasoning if necessary. Put the feta cheese and give it a good mix.
3. Put in the refrigerator for about an hour.
4. Serve and enjoy!!!

Cucumber Salad

Preparation Time: 15 minutes

Total Time: 15 minutes

Serves: 4

Calories: 150 kcal

Ingredients:

- 1 Oz. feta cheese, diced
- 15 Kalamata olives, halved
- 3 Tbsp. extra virgin olive oil
- Salt
- 8 Oz. grape tomatoes, halved
- 8 Oz. English cucumber, sliced
- 1 Oz. red onion, sliced
- Pepper

Cooking Instructions:

1. Except the olive oil, combine together all the ingredients in a small mixing bowl.
2. Put the mixture in the refrigerator. Spray with olive oil alongside with salt and pepper.
3. Serve and enjoy!!!

Tzatziki Sauce

Preparation Time: 14 minutes

Total Time: 14 minutes

Serves: 5

Calories: 44 kcal

Ingredients:

- 1 Tbsp. fresh dill, minced
- 1 Clove garlic, minced
- 1 Cup of Greek yogurt
- 6 Oz. cucumber, grated
- 1 Tbsp. lemon juice

Cooking Instructions:

1. Mix together all the ingredients. Taste for sweetness and put more seasoning if necessary.
2. Serve and enjoy!!!

Homemade Ranch Seasoning

Preparation Time: 14 minutes

Total Time: 14 minutes

Serves: 17

Calories: 5 kcal

Ingredients:

- 1 ½ Tsp. Dried dill
- ½ Tsp. Pink sea salt
- 2 Packets Tru Lemon
- 2 Tbsp. Dried parsley
- 1 Tbsp. Dried chives
- 2 Tsp. Onion powder
- 2 Tsp. Lemon pepper
- 1 Tbsp. Powdered sugar
- 5 Tsp. Granulated garlic

Cooking Instructions:

1. In an electric coffee grinder, put all the ingredients and grind them to powder form.
2. Put the mixture in an air-tight container.
3. Serve and enjoy!!!

Spinach Salad with Warm Bacon Dressing

Preparation Time: 14 minutes

Cook Time: 15 minutes

Total Time: 29 minutes

Serves: 4

Calories: 445 kcal

Ingredients:

- 4 Large Hard boiled eggs, sliced
- 2 Oz. Mushrooms, sliced
- 10 ½ Oz. Baby Spinach
- 8 Oz. Bacon, diced

Warm Bacon Dressing:

- 1 Tbsp. Whole Grain Mustard
- ½ Tsp. Dried tarragon
- Salt
- 2 Tbsp. Shallot, chopped
- ¼ Cup of Bacon grease
- 2 Tbsp. Red wine vinegar
- 1 Tbsp. Sukrin Gold
- Pepper

Cooking Instructions:

1. Put the bacon in a cold pan on a medium heat. Cook for about 6 minutes. Get the bacon out from heat and put bacon grease into a small container.
2. Put the mushrooms to the pan and cook to your desired consistency. Remove and set aside. Sauté the shallots for some few minutes.

3. Reduce the heat and put the vinegar, bacon grease, Sukrin Gold, tarragon, and whole grain mustard, salt and pepper. Give it a good stir.

4. Mix the dressing with the spinach and scoop into 4 serving plates. Top with bacon, eggs, and mushrooms. Serve and enjoy!!!

Honey Mustard Dressing and Dipping Sauce

Preparation Time: 10 minutes

Cook Time: 10 minutes

Total Time: 20 minutes

Serves: 5

Calories: 248 kcal

Ingredients:

- ¼ Tsp. onion powder
- ¼ Tsp. dried tarragon, rubbed between fingers
- 1/8 Tsp. cayenne pepper
- Salt
- ¾ Cup of mayonnaise
- ½ Cup of Dijon Mustard
- ¼ Cup of heavy cream
- 3 Tbsp. Sukrin Icing Sugar
- 1 Tbsp. lemon juice
- ¼ Tsp. granulated garlic powder
- Pepper

Cooking Instructions:

1. Mix together the mustard and mayonnaise in a small mixing bowl. Put the heavy cream.
2. Put the vinegar and the rest of the ingredients. Taste for sweetness. Put in the refrigerator for more thickness.
3. Serve and enjoy!!!

Cauliflower Tabbouleh

Preparation Time: 20 minutes

Cook Time: 2 minutes

Total Time: 22 minutes

Serves: 4

Calories: 143 kcal

Ingredients:

- 2 Tbsp. minced mint
- 2 Tbsp. lemon juice
- ½ Tsp. salt
- ½ Cup of raw cauliflower rice, packed
- ⅓ Cup of raw walnuts
- 1 Large bunch curly parsley, stems removed
- 1 Roma tomato, seeded and diced
- ⅓ Cup minced purple onion
- 4 Tbsp. extra virgin olive oil
- ⅛ Tsp. white pepper

Cooking Instructions:

1. Slice the cauliflower into florets and put into a food blender that is fitted with a metal blade. Blend the cauliflower to be as tiny as rice grain.
2. In order to remove the raw taste from the cauliflower, cook in a pan on a stovetop but do not allow it to be soft.
3. Trim out the parsley stem and slice it and put alongside with walnuts into the food blender and blend to be well chopped.
4. Flip both the cauliflower and parsley mixture into a medium mixing bowl. Put onion, lemon juice, tomato, olive oil, salt and pepper. Give it a good mix. Serve and enjoy!!!

Grilled Chicken Caesar Salad

Preparation Time: 7 minutes

Total Time: 7 minutes

Serves: 4

Calories: 372 kcal

Ingredients:

- ¾ Cup of Lemony Caesar Dressing
- ½ Cup of shredded Parmesan cheese
- Freshly ground pepper
- 1 Lb. romaine lettuce
- 12 Oz. Garlic Herbed Grilled Chicken

Lemony Caesar Dressing:

- 2 Tbsp. fresh lemon juice
- Zest of one lemon
- ¼ Cup of grated Parmesan cheese
- 1 Cup of mayo
- 1 ½ Tsp. anchovy paste
- 1 Clove large garlic
- ¼ Tsp. salt
- 1 ½ Tsp. Dijon mustard
- 1 ½ Tsp. Worcestershire sauce

Cooking Instructions:

1. Put the romaine, chicken and 1 cup of Lemony Caesar Dressing into a large mixing bowl. Give it a good mix. Put the salad into a serving bowl.
2. Put pepper and top with shredded parmesan cheese. Serve and enjoy!!!

KETO DIET BEEF & PORK RECIPES

Lebanese Hashweh Ground Beef and Rice

Preparation Time: 10 minutes

Cook Time: 20 minutes

Total Time: 30 minutes

Serves: 6

Calories: 344 kcal

Ingredients:

- 1 Tsp. Salt
- 1 Tsp. ground Pepper
- 2 Cups of water
- ¼ Mix of cilantro
- 2 Tbsp. Oil or ghee
- ¼ Cup of pine nuts
- 1 Cup of Sliced Onions
- 1 Tbsp. Minced Garlic
- 1 Lb. Lean Ground Beef
- 5 Cardamom Pods
- 1 ½ Tsp. Ground Allspice
- 1 Tsp. ground Cinnamon
- ¼ Ground Nutmeg
- 1 Cup Basmati Rice rinsed and drained

Cooking Instructions:

1. Preheat your oven. Melt butter, put pine nuts and sauté for about 2 minutes.

2. Put minced garlic, onion and give it a good stir. Put ground beef and break it up. Put all other spices. Mix properly and put rice.

3. Serve and enjoy!!!

Beef Kheema Meatloaf

Preparation Time: 10 minutes

Cook Time: 18 minutes

Total Time: 28 minutes

Serves: 4

Calories: 260 kcal

Ingredients:

- 1 Tsp. Turmeric
- 1 Tsp. cayenne
- ½ Tsp. ground cinnamon
- ⅛ Tsp. Ground Cardamom
- 1 Lb. Lean Ground Beef
- 2 Eggs
- 1 Cup of onion diced
- ¼ Cup of cilantro chopped
- 1 Tbsp. minced ginger
- 1 Tbsp. Minced Garlic
- 2 Tsp. Garam Masala
- 1 Tsp. Salt

Cooking instructions:

1. Mix together all ingredients into a large mixing bowl and give it a good stir. ut the meat into a cooking pan.
2. Cook on Air Fryer at 360ºF for about 15 minutes. When the cooking time is up, remove the pan and drain some excess fat and water. Cut into 4 pieces.
3. Serve and enjoy!!!

Beef Shawarma

Preparation Time: 5 minutes

Cook Time: 15 minutes

Total Time: 20 minutes

Serves: 4

Calories: 253 kcal

Ingredients:

- 1 Tsp. Salt
- 8 Oz cabbage
- ¼ Cup of Chopped Parsley
- 2 Tbsp. olive oil
- 1 Lb. Lean Ground Beef
- 1 Cup of onion sliced
- 1 Batch shawarma mix

Cooking Instructions:

1. On a medium heat, heat a sauté pan on a stovetop. Put oil when the cooking pan is hot, followed by ground beef and break the clumps.

2. Put onions and sauté for about 4 minutes. Put shawarma mix and salt. Give it a good stir. Put the shredded cabbage.

3. Put 2 Tbsp. of water and close the lid. Steam the cabbage for about a minute. Open the lid and give it a good stir. Top with parsley.

4. Serve and enjoy!!!

Spicy Ground Pork Stir Fry

Preparation Time: 5 minutes

Cook Time: 15 minutes

Total Time: 20 minutes

Serves: 4

Calories: 415 kcal

Ingredients:

- ½ Cup of Spring onions, chopped
- ½ Cup cilantro, chopped
- 1 Head butter lettuce
- 1 Lb. ground pork
- 1 Tbsp. olive oil
- 2 Tbsp. Sesame Oil
- 1 Tbsp. minced Ginger
- 1 Tbsp. Minced Garlic
- 1 Tbsp. Soy Sauce
- 2 Tsp. Sambal Olek
- 1 Tbsp. Lemon juice
- 3 Green Chili's sliced jalapenos, serranos

Cooking Instructions:

1. Heat oil on a medium high heat on a pan. When the oil is hot, put ginger and garlic and sauté for about 3 seconds.
2. Put the ground pork. Stir properly. Combine together the green onions and cilantro. Keep aside.
3. When the meat is almost done, shift the meat to the sides so you have space in the center. Put the red chili and sliced green.

4. Add sesame oil, soy sauce, the sambal olek. Give it a good mix. Switch off the stove and remove the meat from heat.

5. Put cilantro and chopped green onions. Drizzle the lemon juice and give it a good mix. Serve and enjoy!!!

Mexican Zucchini and Beef

Preparation Time: 5 minutes

Cook Time: 25 minutes

Total Time: 30 minutes

Serves: 6

Calories: 272 kcal

Ingredients:

- ½ Tsp. black pepper
- ½ Tsp. onion powder
- ¼ Tsp. crushed red pepper flakes
- 2 Medium zucchini sliced
- 1 ½ Lbs. ground beef
- 2 Cloves garlic minced
- 10 Oz. Mexican style diced tomatoes with green chili
- 1 Tbsp. chili powder
- 1 Tsp. ground cumin
- 1 Tsp. salt

Cooking Instructions:

1. Sauté the ground beef alongside with garlic, salt, and pepper. On a medium heat, cook the meat to your desired consistency.
2. Put tomatoes alongside with the remaining spices. Close and allow it to simmer on low heat for about 10 minutes.
3. Put the zucchini. Close the lid and cook for about 10 more.
4. Serve and enjoy!!!!

Korean Ground Beef

Preparation Time: 10 minutes

Cook Time: 15 minutes

Total Time: 25 minutes

Serves: 5

Calories: 261 kcal

Ingredients:

- 1/2 Tsp. fresh ginger minced
- 1 Tsp. crushed red pepper
- 1 Bunch green onions sliced
- 1 Tsp. sesame oil or olive oil
- 1 ¼ Lbs. lean ground beef
- 3 Cloves garlic minced
- ½ Tsp. Sweet Leaf stevia drops
- ½ Tsp. blackstrap molasses
- ¼ Cup soy sauce

Cooking Instructions:

1. On a medium heat, heat a large skillet. Put oil and sauté ground beef to become brownish alongside with garlic.
2. Put molasses, stevia, soy sauce, ginger, and red pepper. Allow it to simmer for some minutes.
3. Give it a good mix. Top with sliced green onions.
4. Serve and enjoy!!!

Cheeseburger and Cauliflower

Preparation Time: 15 minutes

Cook Time: 30 minutes

Total Time: 45 minutes

Serves: 6

Calories: 421 kcal

Ingredients:

- 1 Lb. ground meat
- 2 Cup of cauliflower
- 2 Tsp. steak seasoning
- ¼ Cheddar cheese
- 1 Tbsp. butter
- 4 Oz. cream cheese
- 2 Eggs
- ½ Cup of heavy cream
- ½ Cup of cheddar cheese

Cooking Instructions:

1. Preheat oven to 400°F. Put the cauliflower into the microwave for about 5 minutes.
2. Put the beef to a skillet and pour in steak seasoning. Put cream cheese, cauliflower, and ¼ cup of cheddar cheese.
3. Give it a good stir and scoop it into a baking pan. Break the eggs into a small mixing bowl and then put cream and butter.
4. Sprinkle the egg mixture and remaining cheese on top of beef mixture. Bake for 30 minutes.
5. Serve and enjoy!!!

Ground Beef Casserole

Preparation Time: 10 minutes

Cook Time: 40 minutes

Total Time: 50 minutes

Serves: 8

Calories: 334 kcal

Ingredients:

- 1 Egg, beaten
- 1 Cup marinara sauce
- 1 Cup of mozzarella cheese, shredded
- 1 Lb. ground beef
- 1 Tsp. fennel seed
- ½ Tsp. Italian spice seasoning
- 1 Tsp. paprika
- 2 Cups of cauliflower florets
- ½ Cup of Parmesan cheese, grated
- ¼ Cup of cream cheese
- ½ Cup of heavy cream

Cooking Instructions:

1. Preheat oven to 400°F. Put beef, fennel, Italian seasonings and paprika into a skillet and cook to your desired consistency.

2. Put the cauliflower in the microwave and cook for about 5 minutes. When it is brown, put cauliflower mixture and then scoop into a baking pan.

3. Put the cream cheese, cream and Parmesan cheese into the skillet. Give it a good stir, set aside and allow it to cool.

4. Put the egg and then sprinkle on top of the meat and cauliflower mixture. Scoop the sauce into the casserole and then put mozzarella cheese on top.

5. Bake for about 30 minutes.

6. Serve and enjoy!!!

Salad Healthy Taco with Ground Beef

Preparation Time: 10 minutes

Cook Time: 10 minutes

Total Time: 20 minutes

Serves: 6

Calories: 332 kcal

Ingredients:

- ½ Cup Green onions, chopped
- ⅓ Cup Salsa
- ⅓ Cup Sour cream
- 1 Lb. Ground beef
- 1 Tsp. Avocado oil
- 2 Tbsp. Taco seasoning
- 8 Oz. Romaine lettuce, chopped
- 1 ⅓ Cup Grape tomatoes, divided
- ¾ Cup Cheddar cheese, shredded
- 1 Medium Avocado, cubed

Cooking Instructions:

1. On a high heat. Heat oil in a skillet. Put the ground beef. Fry and stir continuously for about 10 minutes.
2. Put taco seasoning into the ground beef and give it a good stir. In a large mixing bowl, mix together all the remaining ingredients.
3. Put the ground beef. Stir well.
4. Serve and enjoy!!!

KETO DIET FISH & SEAFOOD RECIPES

Mini Fish Cakes

Preparation Time: 10 minutes

Cook Time: 25 minutes

Total Time: 35 minutes

Serves: 12 Fishes

Ingredients:

- 1 Lb. white fish, raw and food processed to form a paste
- 2 Cups almond flour
- 4 Eggs, whisked
- Salt and pepper to taste
- 1 Tsp. white wine vinegar
- 1 Tsp. baking powder
- 2 Tbsp. scallions, chopped
- 1 Tsp. garlic powder
- 1 Tbsp. ghee

Cooking Instructions:

1. Preheat oven to 375°F. In a large mixing bowl, combine together all the ingredients together.
2. In a muffin tray, put muffin liners and fill the mixture on each of the muffin. Bake for about 25 minutes.
3. Serve and enjoy!!!

Chinese Petrale Sole with Ginger and Garlic

Preparation Time: 5 minutes

Cook Time: 15 minutes

Total Time: 20 minutes

Serves: 1

Ingredients:

- 1 Tbsp. scallions
- 1 Tsp. ginger, chopped
- 3 Cloves garlic, minced
- 1 Petrale sole fish
- 2 Tbsp. coconut oil
- 3 Tbsp. gluten-free tamari sauce
- 1 Tsp. white wine vinegar

Cooking Instructions:

1. Put the coconut oil into a frying pan. Put the petrale sole into the frying pan and cook both sides for about 5 minutes each.
2. Put the ginger, scallions, garlic, tamari sauce, and vinegar. Dip the fish into the mixture to coat properly.
3. Cook for about 10 minutes.
4. Serve and enjoy!!!

Easy Sardines Salad

Preparation Time: 5 minutes

Total Time: 5 minutes

Serves: 1

Ingredients:

- 1 Tbsp. olive oil
- 1 Tbsp. lemon juice
- Salt
- 1 Can Sardines in olive oil, drained
- ¼ Lb. salad greens
- 1/10 Lb. bacon chopped

Cooking Instructions:

1. Toss the salad greens in the olive oil and lemon juice. Put the bacon and give it a good stir.
2. Put the drained sardines on top and season with salt.
3. Serve and enjoy!!!

Sardines and Onions

Preparation Time: 5 minutes

Total Time: 5 minutes

Serves: 1

Ingredients:

- 1 Tsp. apple cider vinegar
- 1 Tbsp. olive oil
- Salt
- 1 Can sardines in olive oil
- ¼ Red onion, sliced

Cooking Instructions:

1. In a medium mixing bowl, put the sliced onions alongside with olive oil and vinegar.
2. Top with sardines and season with salt to your own taste.
3. Serve and enjoy!!!

Italian Tuna Salad

Preparation Time: 10 minutes

Total Time: 10 minutes

Serves: 4

Ingredients:

- 3 Tbsp. chopped parsley
- ½ Tbsp. lemon juice
- Salt
- 10 Tomatoes, sun dried
- 2 (5 Oz.) Cans of tuna
- 2 Ribs of celery, diced
- 2 Tbsp. of extra virgin olive oil
- 1 Clove of garlic, minced
- Pepper

Cooking Instructions:

1. Soak the tomatoes in warm water for about 30 minutes. Pat dry and slice the tomatoes. Flake the tuna.
2. Combine the tuna along with the sliced tomatoes, extra virgin olive oil, celery, garlic, lemon juice, parsley, salt and pepper.
3. Serve and enjoy!!!

Coconut Tuna Fish Cakes

Preparation Time: 10 minutes

Total Time: 10 minutes

Serves: 2

Ingredients:

- 2 Tbsp. coconut flakes
- 2 Tbsp. olive oil
- ½ Tbsp. salt
- 2 Cans (6 Oz. cans) of tuna
- 1 Tbsp. of fresh basil, chopped
- 1 Jalapeno, diced
- 2 Eggs, whisked
- 2 Tbsp. coconut flour
- 1 Tbsp. coconut oil

Cooking Instructions:

1. Begin to flake the tuna. In a large mixing bowl, combined together all the ingredients.
2. Make the mixture into 4 patties. Put 1 Tbsp. coconut oil into your skillet using a medium heat.
3. Cook the 4 patties for sometimes. Flip over and continue cooking to your desired consistency.
4. Serve and enjoy!!!

Curried Tuna Salad

Preparation Time: 5 minutes

Total Time: 5 minutes

Serves: 1

Ingredients:

- 2 Tbsp. curry powder
- 1 Tsp. dried parsley
- Salt
- 1 Can of tuna, drained and flaked
- 3 Tbsp. mayo
- Pepper

Cooking Instructions:

1. Put the flaked tuna into a mixing bowl alongside with mayo, curry powder, dried parsley, salt and pepper.
2. Give it a good mix. Make spinach salad available.
3. Serve and enjoy!!!

Tomato Tuna Bruschetta

Preparation Time: 10 minutes

Cook Time: 5 minutes

Total Time: 15 minutes

Serves: 4

Ingredients:

- 1 Tbsp. lemon juice
- ¼ Cup parsley, diced
- Salt
- 4 Slices of Keto Bread
- 4 Tbsp. of olive oil
- 1 (6 Oz.) Can of tuna, drained and flaked
- 1 Tomato, de-seeded and diced
- Pepper

Cooking Instructions:

1. Toast 4 slices of keto bread. Sprinkle the slices of Keto bread with olive oil.
2. Combine together the tomato, tuna, parsley, lemon juice, salt and pepper.
3. Serve and enjoy!!!

Pink Peppercorn Smoked Salmon Salad

Preparation Time: 5 minutes

Total Time: 5 minutes

Serves: 1

Ingredients:

- 4 Olives
- 50g Smoked salmon
- 1 Slice of lemon
- 1 Handfuls of arugula salad leaves
- 1 Tsp. of pink peppercorns, crushed

Cooking Instructions:

1. In a small mixing bowl, put the olives and arugula salad leaves. Put the salmon on top of the salad.
2. Pour in the crushed pink peppercorns on top of the salmon. Top with a slice of lemon.
3. Serve and enjoy!!!

Baked Rosemary Salmon

Preparation Time: 5 minutes

Cooking Time: 30 minutes

Total Time: 35 minutes

Serves: 2

Ingredients:

- ¼ Cup of olive oil
- 2 Salmon fillets
- 1 Tbsp. fresh rosemary leaves

Cooking Instructions:

1. Preheat the oven to 350°F. In a small mixing bowl, combine together the rosemary, and olive oil.
2. Brush the salmon fillet with the mixture. Fold each of the fillets in a piece of aluminum foil alongside with some of the remaining mixture.
3. Bake for about 30 minutes.
4. Serve and enjoy!!!

Creamy Salmon Pasta

Preparation Time: 5 minutes

Cooking Time: 5 minutes

Total Time: 10 minutes

Serves: 2

Ingredients:

- 2 Zucchinis spiraled
- ¼ Cup of mayo
- 2 Tbsp. coconut oil
- 8 Oz. of smoked salmon, diced

Cooking Instructions:

1. Melt the coconut in a skillet using medium heat. Put the salmon and sauté for about 3 minutes.
2. Put the zucchini noodles and sauté for another 2 minutes. Put the mayo and give it a good mix. Flip onto 2 serving plates.
3. Serve and enjoy!!!

Bacon-Wrapped Salmon

Preparation Time: 10 minutes

Cooking Time: 20 minutes

Total Time: 30 minutes

Serves: 2

Ingredients:

- 2 Tbsp. of Basil Pesto
- 2 Tbsp. of Paleo mayo
- Salt
- 2 Filets of salmon, fresh
- 4 Slices of bacon
- 1 Tbsp. of olive oil
- Freshly ground black pepper

Cooking Instructions:

1. Preheat the oven to 350°F. Pat dry the salmon and fold it with the bacon.
2. Put in a tray that is oven-safe. Sprinkle with olive oil and bake for about 20 minutes.
3. In a small mixing bowl, mix together the mayonnaise, pesto salt and freshly ground black pepper.
4. Serve and enjoy!!!

Salmon Curry

Preparation Time: 10 minutes

Cooking Time: 15 minutes

Total Time: 25 minutes

Serves: 2

Ingredients:

- 1 Lb. of raw salmon, diced
- 2 Tbsp. coconut oil
- Salt
- ½ Medium onion, chopped
- 2 Cups of green beans, diced
- ½ Tbsp. curry powder
- 1 Tsp. garlic powder
- Cream from the top of 1 can of coconut milk
- 2 Cups of bone broth
- Pepper
- 2 Tbsp. basil, chopped

Cooking Instructions:

1. Put coconut oil into a skillet and sauté the onion. Put the green beans and sauté for some few minutes.
2. Put broth and boil it. Put the garlic powder, curry powder, salmon, coconut cream, salt and pepper.
3. Allow it to simmer for about 5 minutes. Top with basil.
4. Serve and enjoy!!!

Garlic Shrimp Caesar Salad

Preparation Time: 15 minutes

Cooking Time: 10 minutes

Total Time: 25 minutes

Serves: 4

Ingredients:

For the shrimp:

- 3 Tbsp. garlic powder
- 1 Tbsp. onion powder
- Salt
- 1 Lb. shrimp
- 2 Tbsp. olive oil
- 1 Tbsp. lemon juice
- Pepper

For the salad:

- 1 Head romaine lettuce, chopped
- 1 Cucumber, chopped

For the dressing:

- 1 Tbsp. fresh lemon juice
- 2 Tsp. garlic powder
- Salt
- 1 Tsp. Dijon mustard
- ¼ Cup Paleo mayo
- Pepper

For garnish:

- 1 Tbsp. parsley, chopped
- 1 Tbsp. sliced almonds

Cooking Instructions:

1. Preheat oven to 400ºF. Combine together the olive oil, shrimp, lemon juice, garlic, onion powder, salt and pepper.

2. Put the mixture on a baking pan and bake for about 10 minutes.

3. For the salad dressing, put mayo, mustard, lemon juice, garlic powder, salt and pepper into a food blender and give it a good blend.

4. Give the dressing a good toss alongside with the cucumber, lettuce, and roasted shrimp. Top with the sliced almonds and parsley.

5. Serve and enjoy!!!

Shrimp Cocktail

Preparation Time: 5 minutes

Cooking Time: 5 minutes

Total Time: 10 minutes

Serves: 2

Ingredients:

- Pinch Italian seasoning
- 2 Tsp. lemon juice
- Lemon wedges
- 2 Tbsp. Keto Tomato Ketchup
- 2 Tbsp. mayo
- Salt
- Freshly ground black pepper
- 8 Oz. cooked, peeled prawns
- 1 Cup of iceberg lettuce, shredded
- ½ Large avocado, diced

Cooking Instructions:

1. Mix together the tomato ketchup, mayo, salt and pepper. Dip the prawns into the prepared sauce for proper coating.
2. Cut the avocado and lettuce into 2 bowls. Top with the prawns and squeeze 1 Tsp. of lemon juice into the 2 cups.
3. Pour in lemon wedges and pinch of Italian seasoning.
4. Serve and enjoy!!!

KETO DIET VEGETARIAN & VEGAN RECIPES

Cauliflower Toast

Preparation Time: 15 minutes

Cooking Time: 45 minutes

Total Time: 60 minutes

Serves: 4

Ingredients:

- 1 Medium head cauliflower, grated
- 1 Large egg
- ½ Cup of shredded Cheddar
- 1 Tsp. garlic powder
- Kosher salt
- Freshly ground black pepper

Cooking Instructions:

1. Preheat oven to 425ºF. Place parchment paper on a baking pan. In a large mixing bowl, put your grated cauliflower.
2. Put it in the microwave on high heat for about 8 minutes. Properly drain to dry using paper towels.
3. Put cheddar, egg, garlic powder, salt and pepper to the bowl containing cauliflower. Give it a good stir.
4. On the baking pan, make the cauliflower into toast shapes and bake for about 20 minutes.
5. Flip onto a serving plate and top with mashed avocado, bacon, or lettuce.
6. Serve and enjoy!!!

Baked Egg Avocado Boats

Preparation Time: 10 minutes

Cooking Time: 20 minutes

Total Time: 30 minutes

Serves: 4

Ingredients:

- Freshly ground black pepper
- 3 Slices bacon
- Freshly chopped chives
- 2 Ripe avocados, halved and pitted
- 4 Large eggs
- Kosher salt

Cooking Instructions:

1. Preheat oven to 350°F. In a baking pan, put avocados, and then beat eggs into a small mixing bowl.
2. Remove one egg yolk into each of the avocado half. Scoop the egg white into the avocado. DO not let it spill over.
3. Put salt and pepper. Bake for about 20 minutes. Cook bacon in a large skillet on a medium heat for about 8 minutes.
4. Flip onto a plate lined with paper towel and slice. Top with chives and bacon.
5. Serve and enjoy!!!

Creamy Avocado Dip

Preparation Time: 5 minutes

Total Time: 5 minutes

Serves: 1

Ingredients:

- 2 Tbsp. hemp seeds
- ½ Tbsp. pure vanilla extract
- Pinch kosher salt
- ¾ Cup of almond milk
- ½ Cup of ice
- 2 Tbsp. almond butter
- 2 Tbsp. unsweetened cocoa powder
- 3 Tbsp. keto-friendly sugar substitute
- 1 Tbsp. chia seeds

Cooking Instructions:

1. In a food blender, mix together all the ingredients and give it a good blend.
2. Put into a glass and top with hemp seeds and chia.
3. Serve and enjoy!!!

Jalapeño Popper Bread

Preparation Time: 15 minutes

Cooking Time: 25 minutes

Total Time: 40 minutes

Serves: 16

Ingredients:

- ¾ Tsp. kosher salt
- ½ Cup of shredded cheddar
- 1 Jalapeño, sliced
- Cooking spray
- 6 Egg whites
- ¾ Tsp. cream of tartar
- 4 Egg yolks
- ¼ (8 Oz.) Block cream cheese, softened
- 1 Tsp. garlic powder

Cooking Instructions:

1. Preheat oven to 300°F. Place parchment paper on a baking pan and sprinkle with cooking spray.
2. Break egg whites with cream of tartar in a large mixing bowl using a hand mixer. Give it a good mix.
3. Break cream cheese, egg yolks, garlic powder, and salt into another mixing bowl using a hand mixer.
4. Give it a good mix. Fold in egg whites and cheddar. Put ¼ cup onto already prepared baking pan.
5. Top each with jalapeño slices. Bake for about 25 minutes. Serve and enjoy!!!

Triple Berry Smoothie

Preparation Time: 5 minutes

Total Time: 5 minutes

Serves: 4

Ingredients:

- 2 Cup of coconut milk
- 1 Cup of baby spinach
- 1 ½ Cup of frozen strawberries
- 1 Cup of frozen blackberries

Cooking Instructions:

1. Mix together all the ingredients in a food processor and give it a good blend.
2. Put into about 4 cups.
3. Serve and enjoy!!!

Almond Flour Waffles

Preparation Time: 10 minutes

Total Time: 10 minutes

Serves: 2

Ingredients:

- 2 Tsp. pure vanilla extract
- Cooking spray
- Sugar-free maple syrup
- 4 Large eggs, separated
- 2 Cup of almond flour
- ¼ Cup of granulated swerve
- 2 Tsp. baking powder
- 1 Tsp. kosher salt
- ½ Cup of butter
- ½ Cup of almond butter

Cooking Instructions:

1. Preheat waffle iron to high. Mix together stevia, almond flour, baking powder, and salt in a large mixing bowl. Give it a good mix.

2. Melt the butter and almond butter in a small bowl that is microwave-safe. Pour in the melted butter, yolks and vanilla. Give it a good stir.

3. Break the egg whites into a large mixing using a hand mixer Give it a good stir and fold whites into batter.

4. Pour cooking spray on the waffle iron and the put half of the batter into the waffle iron and cook for about 5 minutes.

5. Flip onto a serving plate and do the same to any remaining batter. Top with maple syrup. Serve and enjoy!!!

Chocolate Protein Shake

Preparation Time: 5 minutes

Total Time: 5 minutes

Serves: 1

Ingredients:

- 2 Tbsp. hemp seeds
- ½ Tbsp. pure vanilla extract
- Pinch kosher salt
- ¾ Cup of almond milk
- ½ Cup of ice
- 3 Tbsp. keto-friendly sugar substitute
- 1 Tbsp. chia seeds
- 2 Tbsp. almond butter
- 2 Tbsp. unsweetened cocoa powder

Cooking Instructions:

1. In a food processor, mix together all the ingredients and give it a good blend.
2. Put the blended mixture into a glass. Top with hemp seeds and chia.
3. Serve and enjoy!!!

Fat Bombs

Preparation Time: 5 minutes

Total Time: 5 minutes

Serves: 16

Ingredients:

- ¼ Tsp. kosher salt
- ½ Cup of keto-friendly dark chocolate chips
- 8 Oz. cream cheese, softened
- ½ Cup of keto-friendly peanut butter
- ¼ Cup of coconut oil

Cooking Instructions:

1. Place parchment paper on a baking pan. Mix together peanut butter, cream cheese, ¼ cup coconut oil, and salt.

2. Mix the mixture thoroughly using hand mixer. Put the mixture in the refrigerator for about 15 minutes.

3. Immediately you observed that the peanut butter mixture has hardened, use a spoon to create some balls to the size of tablespoon.

4. Put in the refrigerator again for about5 minutes. Mix together chocolate chips and remaining coconut oil in a small bowl that is microwave-safe.

5. Put in the microwave for 30 second intervals. Sprinkle on top of peanut butter balls and return it to the refrigerator for about 5 minutes.

6. Serve and enjoy!!!

Easy Cereal

Preparation Time: 10 minutes

Cooking Time: 25 minutes

Total Time: 35 minutes

Serves: 3

Ingredients:

- ½ Tsp. kosher salt
- 1 Large egg white
- ¼ Cup of melted coconut oil
- Cooking spray
- 1 Cup of almonds, chopped
- 1 Cup of walnuts, chopped
- 1 Cup of unsweetened coconut flakes
- ¼ Cup of sesame seeds
- 2 Tbsp. flax seeds
- 2 Tbsp. chia seeds
- ½ Tsp. ground clove
- 1 ½ Tsp. ground cinnamon
- 1 Tsp. pure vanilla extract

Cooking Instructions:

1. Preheat oven to 350°F. Spray your cooking spray in your baking pan.
2. Combine together walnuts, almonds, coconut flakes, flax seeds, and chia seeds, cloves, cinnamon, vanilla, sesame seeds, and salt in a large mixing bowl.
3. Break the egg white into granola. Put coconut oil and give it a good mix. Put the mixture into the baking pan in an equal layer.

4. Bake for about 25 minutes.
5. Serve and enjoy!!!

Cheesy Cauliflower Breadsticks

Preparation Time: 10 minutes

Cooking Time: 35 minutes

Total Time: 45 minutes

Serves: 1

Ingredients:

- Freshly ground black pepper
- Pinch of crushed red pepper flakes
- 2 Tsp. Freshly Chopped Parsley
- Marinara
- 1 Large head cauliflower
- 2 Large eggs
- 2 Cloves garlic, minced
- ½ Tsp. dried oregano
- 3 Cup Of shredded mozzarella, cut
- ½ Cup of grated Parmesan
- Kosher salt

Cooking Instructions:

1. Preheat oven to 425°F. Place parchment paper on a baking pan. Grate the cauliflower in a food blender.
2. Flip the grated cauliflower into a large mixing bowl alongside with garlic, eggs, oregano, Parmesan, 1 cup of mozzarella, salt and pepper.
3. Mix properly. Flip the dough onto the baking pan and pat into a crust. Bake for about 25 minutes.
4. Put the remaining crushed red pepper flakes, mozzarella, and parsley. Bake for about 10 minutes more. Serve and enjoy!!!

Bell Pepper Nachos

Preparation Time: 15 minutes

Cooking Time: 20 minutes

Total Time: 35 minutes

Serves: 6

Ingredients:

- ½ Cup of pickled jalapeño slices
- ½ Cup of sour cream
- 1 Tbsp. milk
- Lime wedges
- 4 Bell peppers, sliced
- 2 Tbsp. extra-virgin olive oil
- ¼ Tsp. garlic powder
- Kosher salt
- Freshly ground black pepper
- 1 ½ Cup of shredded Monterey Jack
- 1 ½ Cup of shredded cheddar
- 1 Cup of guacamole
- 1 Cup of pico de gallo salsa
- ½ Tsp. ground cumin
- ½ Tsp. chili powder

Cooking Instructions:

1. Preheat oven to 425°F. Place foil with 2 baking pans. Share the bell peppers into the two baking pans.

2. Put cumin, olive oil, chili powder, garlic powder, salt and pepper. In a single layer, place the wedges on the baking pans.

3. Bake for about 10 minutes. Top with cheddar and Monterey Jack. Bake for another 10 minutes. Top with salsa, guacamole, and pickled jalapeños.

4. Mix together sour cream and milk in a small mixing bowl and sprinkle on top of bell peppers. Squeeze a lime wedge on top.

5. Serve and enjoy!!!

Avocado Pesto and Spaghetti Squash

Preparation Time: 10 minutes

Cooking Time: 45 minutes

Total Time: 55 minutes

Serves: 2

Ingredients:

- 1 Clove garlic
- ¼ Cup of pecorino cheese
- 3 Tbsp. olive oil
- 1 Spaghetti squash
- 1 Ripe avocado
- ½ Cup of walnuts
- 1 Cup of packed fresh basil
- ½ Lemon

Cooking Instruction:

1. Preheat your oven to 400°F. Slice your spaghetti squash into 2 equal parts.
2. Get the seed out, rub with olive oil, season with salt and pepper. Cook on a baking pan for about 45 minutes.
3. Put avocado, basil, olive oil, walnuts, garlic, lemon and salt in a food blender and give it a good blend.
4. When the cooking time is up, turn each half of the spaghetti scraping the inside with a fork. Top with avocado pesto.
5. Serve and enjoy!!!

Cumin Cilantro Cauliflower Rice

Preparation Time: 10 minutes

Cooking Time: 15 minutes

Total Time: 25 minutes

Serves: 2

Ingredients:

- 1 Medium cauliflower head, riced
- ½ Cup minced cilantro
- Zest and juice from 2 limes
- 2 Tablespoons coconut oil
- 1 Small white onion, diced
- 3 Garlic cloves, minced
- 1 ½ Tsp. kosher salt
- 1 Tsp. cumin

Cooking Instructions:

1. In a large skillet, put oil on a medium heat. Put the onions. Stir cook for about 10 minutes. Put salt, garlic, and cumin.
2. Give it a good mix and cook for about 30 seconds. Put the riced cauliflower. Mix well and cook for about 5 minutes.
3. Put the lime zest, cilantro, and juice.
4. Serve and enjoy!!!

Easy Roasted Broccoli

Preparation Time: 10 minutes

Cooking Time: 20 minutes

Total Time: 30 minutes

Serves: 4

Ingredients:

- ¼ Tsp. red chili flakes pepper, crushed
- Juice of half a lemon
- 2 Tbsp. olive oil, chopped
- 10 Oz. broccoli florets
- ½ Tsp. salt

Cooking Instructions:

1. Preheat the oven to 400° F. Pour 1 Tbsp. olive oil on a cooking pan.
2. Mix together the broccoli, salt, remaining oil, crushed red chili flakes, and pepper in a large mixing bowl.
3. On an oven mitt, remove the cooking pan out of the oven and put the broccoli in a single layer.
4. Cook for about 15 minutes, Turn over and cook for another 5 minutes.
5. Get the cooking pan out from the oven and pour the lemon juice on top of the broccoli.
6. Serve and enjoy!!!

Cheesy Garlic Roasted Asparagus

Preparation Time: 10 minutes

Cooking Time: 20 minutes

Total Time: 15 minutes

Serves: 4

Ingredients:

- ¾ Tsp. kosher salt
- ¼ Tsp. fresh cracked black pepper
- 1 ¼ Cup of shredded mozzarella cheese
- 1 Lb. asparagus spears, woody ends removed
- 3 Tbsp. olive oil
- 1 Tbsp. minced garlic

Cooking Instructions:

1. Preheat oven to 425°F. Pour nonstick cooking oil spray on a baking pan. Place the asparagus on the baking pan and keep aside.
2. Combine together olive oil, garlic, salt and pepper in a small mixing bowl. Sprinkle the olive oil mixture on top of the asparagus and mix properly.
3. Top with mozzarella cheese and bake for about 15 minutes. Broil for about 5 minutes.
4. Serve and enjoy!!!

KETO DIET APPETIZER RECIPES

Crunchy Rosemary Crackers

Preparation Time: 10 minutes

Cooking Time: 30 minutes

Total Time: 40 minutes

Serves: 15 crackers

Ingredients:

- ½ Cup of pecans
- 1 Cup of pumpkin seeds
- ¼ Cup of flax meal
- 1 Large whole egg
- 1 Tbsp. olive oil
- 4 Tbsp. water
- ½ Tsp. salt
- ¼ Tsp. pepper
- 2 Tbsp. rosemary, chopped
- ½ Tsp. garlic powder
- ½ Cup of almonds

Cooking Instructions:

1. Preheat oven to 325°F. Place parchment paper on a baking pan.
2. In a small mixing bowl, break in the egg, put olive oil, water, salt, pepper, garlic powder, and rosemary.
3. In a large food blender, put nuts and seeds and give it a good blend. Put flax meal. Mix well and put liquid mixture.
4. Wrap the mixture on a parchment paper. Slice into equal portions and place in a baking pan. Bake for about 30 minutes. Serve and enjoy!!!

Macadamia Nut Hummus

Preparation Time: 5 minutes

Total Time: 5 minutes

Serves: 8

Ingredients:

- 2 Tbsp. tahini
- Pinch cayenne pepper
- Sea salt
- 1 Cup raw macadamia nuts, soaked in water for 24 hours, drained
- 3 Cloves garlic
- 3 Tbsp. fresh lemon juice
- 3 Tbsp. water
- Freshly ground pepper

Cooking Instructions:

1. In a food blender, put all the ingredients and give it a good blend.
2. Serve and enjoy!!!

Cauliflower Mac and Cheese

Preparation Time: 10 minutes

Cooking Time: 30 minutes

Total Time: 40 minutes

Serves: 3

Ingredients:

- 1 ¼ Tsp. paprika
- 8 Oz. heavy cream
- 4 Oz. sharp cheddar, shredded
- 4 Oz. fontina, shredded
- 2 Oz. cream cheese
- 1 Tsp. salt
- ½ Tsp. black pepper
- 1 Large head of cauliflower

Cooking Instructions:

1. Preheat oven to 375°F. Put non cooking spray into the baking pan. Slice cauliflower into small pieces.
2. Simmer for about 5 minutes. Get it out from heat, drain and pat dry using paper towel.
3. Mix together heavy cream, cheeses, cream cheese, salt, pepper, and paprika in a small pot. Heat and stir properly.
4. Put cauliflower to cheese mixture and give it a good mix. Flip into baking pan and bake for about 30 minutes.
5. Serve and enjoy!!!

Cheesy Buffalo Chicken Dip

Preparation Time: 5 minutes

Cooking Time: 6 hours

Total Time: 6 hours 5 minutes

Serves: 2

Ingredients:

- 1 Tsp. garlic powder
- 2 Oz. cream cheese
- 1 Cup of cheddar cheese
- 8 Chicken thighs
- 1 Small yellow onion
- ½ Cup of Frank's Buffalo Sauce
- ½ Tsp. salt
- ¼ Tsp. pepper
- 2 Tsp. paprika

Cooking Instructions:

1. Put spices, onion, and buffalo sauce to a Crock Pot. Give it a good mix. Put the chicken thighs.
2. Cover and cook on high heat for about 6 hours. When the cooking time is up open and shred the chicken using two forks.
3. Put cheddar cheese and cream cheese.
4. Serve and enjoy!!!

Chipotle Red Pepper Cheese Dip

Preparation Time: 10 minutes

Cooking Time: 15 minutes

Total Time: 25 minutes

Serves: 4

Ingredients:

- 3 Medium red peppers, seeds and stalks removed
- 1 Tbsp. olive oil
- ½ Cup of sun-dried tomatoes
- ½ Cup of full-fat cream cheese
- 1 Garlic clove, minced
- 1 Tsp. paprika
- Pinch of dried chipotle
- Sea salt

Cooking Instructions:

1. Preheat the oven to 400°F. Chop the peppers and put on a baking sheet. Put 1 Tbsp. olive oil and roast in the oven for about 15 minutes.
2. Put in a zip-lock bag and allow it to steam 5 minutes. Remove the skins. In a small mixing bowl.
3. Put the sun dried tomatoes, peppers, chipotle or chili, paprika, garlic, cream cheese, and salt. Blitz with a hand blender.
4. Serve and enjoy!!!

Epic Charcuterie Board

Preparation Time: 20 minutes

Cooking Time: 20 minutes

Total Time: 40 minutes

Serves: 5

Ingredients:

- 20 Pickled asparagus spears
- ¼ Cup of sauerkraut
- ¼ Cup of stone ground mustard
- 1 Sleeve low carb crackers
- 6 Oz. sliced prosciutto
- 6 Oz. genoa salami
- 5 Oz. spicy capocollo
- 4 Oz. herbed chevre
- 6 Oz. sliced manchego
- 5 Oz. sliced peppercorn white cheddar
- 4 Oz. garlic white cheddar
- ¼ Cup of Olive Salad
- ½ Cup of pitted Kalamata olives
- ¼ Roasted red peppers
- ½ Cup of Low Carb Pickled Red Onion
- ¼ Cup of Sugar-Free Dried Cranberries
- 1/2 Cup of mixed nuts
- ½ Cup of fresh blackberries

- 10 Strawberries hulled and halved
- 5 Pepperoncini's
- ½ Cup of pickled artichoke hearts
- 10 Garlic stuffed green olives

Cooking Instructions:

1. Combine all the ingredients together.
2. Serve and enjoy!!!

General Tso's Meatballs

Preparation Time: 15 minutes

Cooking Time: 20 minutes

Total Time: 35 minutes

Serves: 4

Ingredients:

For the Meatballs:

- ¼ Cup of almond flour
- 1 Egg
- Light flavored oil
- 1 Lb. ground turkey or chicken
- 2 Tbsp. minced ginger
- ¼ Cup of scallions, chopped
- 1 Tsp. garlic powder

For the Sauce:

- ½ Tsp. xanthan gum
- ¼ Cup of scallions, chopped
- 5 Small dried chilies, seeded and chopped
- ½ Tsp. sesame oil
- 3 Tbsp. rice wine vinegar
- 3 Tbsp. soy sauce
- ¼ Cup of water
- 3 Tbsp. sugar substitute

Cooking Instructions:

1. In a medium mixing bowl, mix together all the meatball ingredients and give it a good stir.

2. Make 16 balls and sauté in oil on a medium heat to your desired consistency.

3. In a small saucepan, mix together the vinegar, sesame oil, GF soy sauce, water, sugar substitute, and xanthan gum.

4. Give it a good stir. Put the scallions and chili pepper and boil. Allow it to simmer for about 5 minutes.

5. Put the cooked meatballs to the sauce and mix well.

6. Serve and enjoy!!!

Pepperoni Pizza Stuffed Mushrooms

Preparation Time: 5 minutes

Cooking Time: 15 minutes

Total Time: 20 minutes

Serves: 4

Calories: 70 kcal

Ingredients:

- 1 Cup of mozzarella cheese
- Freshly ground black pepper
- 1 Fresh basil leaf chopped
- 15 Large mushrooms cleaned and stems removed
- 2 Mini pepperoni links sliced
- ¼ Cup of pizza sauce

Cooking Instructions:

1. Preheat oven to 450°F. Place the mushrooms in a skillet.
2. Fill 2 Tsp. of the pizza sauce on each of the mushroom. Top with 3 pepperoni slices and 2 Tbsp. of mozzarella cheese.
3. Bake for about 18 minutes. Put freshly ground black pepper and garnish with basil.
4. Serve and enjoy!!!

Cheese Tray-Cheddar, Monterey Jack, and Cream Cheese Platter

Preparation Time: 20 minutes

Total Time: 20 minutes

Serves: 16

Calories: 189 kcal

Ingredients:

- 3 Garlic Clove minced
- 1 Tsp. Sugar
- 1 Tsp. Basil chopped
- Salt
- 8 Oz. Block Cheddar
- 8 Oz. Block Cream Cheese
- ½ Cup of Olive Oil
- ½ Cup of White Wine Vinegar
- 2 Oz. Jar Pimento drained
- 3 Tbsp. Fresh Parsley, chopped
- 3 Tbsp. Fresh Green Onion, chopped
- Pepper
- 8 Oz. Block Monterey Jack Cheese

Cooking Instructions:

1. Slice the cheese into 4 quarters. Let all the cheese slices be the same size and shape.
2. Place the cheese slices on a shallow serving plate standing each slice on its edge.
3. Combine together the remaining marinade ingredients in a jar.

4. Give it a good mix and pour the mixture on top of cheese. Allow it to marinate for about 8 hours.

5. Serve and enjoy!!!

Eggplant Tomato Mini Pizza

Preparation Time: 10 minutes

Cooking Time: 15 minutes

Total Time: 25 minutes

Serves: 8

Calories: 74 kcal

Ingredients:

- ½ Tsp. basil
- ½ Tsp. oregano
- ½ Cup of mozzarella cheese
- 2 Small eggplants
- 2 Tbsp. olive oil
- ½ Tsp. salt
- Dash ground black pepper
- 2 Medium tomatoes

Cooking Instructions:

1. Preheat oven to 425° F. Rub olive oil, salt and pepper on both side of the eggplant. Bake for about 10 minutes. Flip over halfway.
2. Put 1 tomato slice on each eggplant slice. Pour basil and oregano top of the eggplant slice alongside with shredded mozzarella cheese.
3. Bake for about 5 minutes.
4. Serve and enjoy!!!

Creamy Herb and Cucumber Dressing

Preparation Time: 10 minutes

Total Time: 10 minutes

Serves: 10

Calories: 45 kcal

Ingredients:

- 1 Tbsp. freshly squeezed lemon juice
- ¾ Tsp. dried dill
- 2 Green onions chopped
- Salt
- 1 Cup of chopped cucumber
- ¾ Cup of sour cream
- 1 Tbsp. heaping mayonnaise
- Pepper

Cooking instructions:

1. In a food blender, put all the ingredients. Give it a good blend.
2. Serve and enjoy!!!